Neil We

# Cribs For Victory

The Untold Story of Bletchley Park's Secret Room

Edited by

## Joss Pearson

British Library Cataloguing in Publication Data.
A catalogue record for this book is available from the British Library.

ISBN 9780955954184

Published by
Polperro Heritage Press,
Clifton-upon-Teme, Worcestershire
WR6 6EN
United Kingdom
www.polperropress.co.uk

Cover design
Steve Bowgen

Printed in Great Britain by
Orphans Press, Leominster
United Kingdom

# CONTENTS

from *Satire III*
by
John Donne

'... though truth and falsehood be
Near twins, yet truth a little elder is;
Be busy to seek her; believe me this,
He's not of none, nor worst, that seeks the best.
To adore, or scorn an image, or protest,
May all be bad; doubt wisely; in strange way
To stand inquiring right, is not to stray;
To sleep, or run wrong, is. On a huge hill,
Cragged and steep, Truth stands, and he that will
Reach her, about must and about must go,
And what the hill's suddenness resists, win so.'

*This book is dedicated to Neil Webster who was always in pursuit of truth.*

# Foreword

This book is published posthumously – more than a quarter of a century after it was first written by my father, Major Neil Leslie Webster, and more than 20 years after his death. It is his first-hand account of his wartime life from 1939 to1946 and his own and his colleagues' work in intelligence. He had been recruited by MI8 in April 1940, lifted out of his enlistment in the London Scottish to join the early members in Caxton Street of the Central Party. It was in Caxton St, as he describes in this book, that the idea was born of 'fusion'– integrating the knowledge from signals intelligence with decodes from cryptography. The Central Party moved to Harpenden, and the unit my father worked in was from then on known as the 'Fusion Room' - continuing in Beaumanor and finally in Bletchley Park (BP) where, as a Major, he was liaison officer between signals intelligence and cryptographers, in what is now known as SIXTA. The Fusion Room in BP was the central unit where decrypted German messages obtained from Hut 6 were compared with the corresponding data extracted by the log readers from the daily radio traffic between enemy stations, thus enabling a complete wartime picture of the enemy order of battle to be constructed. The Fusion Room grew from a small beginning in 1940 until, by the end of the war at BP in 1945, it numbered over two dozen men and women, including a few American army officers who had arrived in 1943. Because my dad's role was liaison between traffic analysis and cryptography, he was centrally involved in the search for 'cribs' – short pieces of enciphered text where the meaning is either known or can be guessed, which allow the whole cipher to be broken. He had a roving brief, to help Hut 6 people to break ciphers, especially Enigma so that the information could reach Hut 3 intelligence. His book describes this intensive search in detail, the intellectual and technical challenge, the personal stories, the setbacks and the triumphs.

Security clearance and permission to publish this material was only given in 2010, at the family's request. In this foreword I tell the story of how this occurred, from a daughter's point of view - drawing both on childhood recollections and on my recent adult involvement in the book's publication.

I was born in December 1941 in the middle of World War 2, in Loughborough. When I later asked my mum, "Why Loughborough?" I was told that we were living at the time in Woodhouse Eaves in a rented cottage, because "Dad was working nearby"; later they said "working in Beaumanor". All I remember of Woodhouse Eaves, being under three years old when we left, is the cottage garden where I played with my older brother Andrew and a white windmill on a hill and Dad in uniform, occasionally present. My mother, born a Heygate, relates in her unpublished autobiography how Woodhouse Eaves turned out coincidentally to be the seat of a high-class branch of the Heygate family and how her beloved grandmother (also a Heygate), who had raised her and was living with them at the time, began proudly boasting in the village about "my grandson-in-law, you know, in intelligence - very hush-hush" - until Dad expressed concern, whereat she removed herself back to Cheshire.

After Woodhouse Eaves, Mum and us kids lived for a time in 1943 at our Webster grandparents in Cheltenham, with visits from Dad whose unit had moved to Bletchley Park. Apparently he rode a motorbike down from BP - which must have been quite a sight since Dad was a small man, dashing and handsome with a charming quizzical smile, farseeing Scottish blue eyes and unruly hair. Even in wartime, Cheltenham was pretty grand, with only occasional soldiers marching past and us kids joyfully shouting "Got any gum, chum?" while hanging on the gate, so that the GIs showered us with packets of gum - wealth beyond our dreams! From the grandparents we learned more about family history. Dad too had been raised mainly by grandparents. He was the favourite grandson of the Indian novelist Flora Annie Steel, and a large portrait of her and many Indian curios were in the house. Dad's mother was Flora Annie's daughter - known to us as 'Aunt Mabel', and his father, 'Uncle Jack' Webster, was retired from a lifetime of civil service in India, winner of the Star of India.

Then in 1944 we moved to Bletchley, to a 2-up 2-down dark little house in Fenny Stratford. I remember it very well. By this time there were three of us, elder brother, baby brother, and me. A neighbour's teenage daughter, Joy, occasionally 'minded' and played with us. The back of the house had a straight strip of garden with a path down the middle, leading to a field hedge, and beside the path was the air-raid shelter, dank and smelly, and in the field hedge were blackberries and beyond, a bull. We three slept in a little room at the top of the steep stairs, with tin trays tied around our cots 'to protect against shrapnel' or flying glass. In the back garden was a bucket of sand, as Joy said "for incendiaries". I hardly knew about the war. Dad cycled to work nearby in 'the Bletchley Park' which was apparently a 'Hoover factory' – though we kids knew the grown-ups didn't believe this. I don't remember ever visiting the Park, but Mum used to push the big pram with us up the road that went under the railway arch towards BP. And we used to collect blackberries from the banks on the way.

Occasionally in the evenings tall men and clever women called at the little house for supper or drinks and we kids were banished upstairs. I remember the American, Bill Bijur who called the flowers round the weedy air-raid shelter 'parpees' however much I insisted they were 'poppies'. Dad liked the Americans - he had spent some years in the States before the War.  On one evening party occasion (I was told later) I came to the top of the stairs and winningly said "Come on up soldier" to a visitor - to the consternation of parents and the delight of the invitee! Apparently on another evening, when Alan Turing was there for supper, Andrew was making a fuss and Malcolm Spooner, the mathematician who was also present, got down on his knees to talk to him. "The world looks pretty alarming from down here, you know!" he said. By 1945, my brother and I were exploring Fenny - the canal and timber yard (forbidden territory) and the sweet shop up a lot of steps on the main crossroads to Bletchley (also forbidden) and the little green patch nearby. My brother remembers German prisoners of war working on the road outside our house. One of them pointed his shovel at Andrew and made gun-firing noises for a joke - but Andrew set up a terrified scream bringing mum running. Once, out the back, a German fighter plane, astray over Bletchley, buzzed the house - apparently chasing me up the path - and I ran to the kitchen in terror. Otherwise, I remember the VE Day party and fete, when we kids were dressed up as elves and processed excitedly around Fenny with quite a crowd.

When the war was mostly over the family moved to Kent, after a brief return to the grandparents in Cheltenham for us kids. Then I became more aware of the war - retrospectively. My dad had bought an ex-requisitioned big house, where army personnel had ridden motorbikes all over the garden, flattening it, and parked bicycles in the house knocking it about. But by the time we children got there, in 1946 my indomitable mum had created order and charm. Upstairs in the back in a small room with a desk, a brown carpet and a war-issue filing cabinet my dad had his study. It was the first time he was at home for an extended period, and I got to know him. He had finished his history of the work of his group at Bletchley and I remember the mysterious large brown waxy punched cards in the filing cabinet.. At some point after we had settled in, I came up to his study to call him for tea and found him sitting with an air of weary distress. He had just heard the latest figures from Hiroshima.

The other post-war impact on our lives came more slowly. My mother began taking in children from divided or absent families, and we kids grew up in a tribe, with responsibility for looking after and 'settling in' lost and confused children into our large house and rambling garden. Gradually over the years the 'Hoover factory' was forgotten and replaced with 'Dad's work at Bletchley' and then 'intelligence'. Then came the time my elder brother and I signed something called 'The Official Secrets Act', which meant promising not to talk about Dad's work at Bletchley. Later still, we knew more about it. At various times when I was grown up, he tried to explain how the Enigma machine worked – but I found it too daunting for my low grasp of maths and my younger brother, a clever lad, scoffed at my dimness. I even once, much later, asked him to write it up for a case study for a possible book on mind games – which he did, but I still was foxed. Reading *Cribs for Victory* now, I realise that I did perhaps understand a bit – and that many of the names are very familiar too. These were the legendary names of my childhood, whose mention made my dad's eyes twinkle, as we kids grew up in the post-War world.

For all these years, my father had been working at the Central Office of Information (COI) in London. He was responsible for the annual preparation and publication of The Britain Handbook. The work involved co-ordinating the input of many different bodies, endless circulation of drafts and endless committees, requiring the same skill with diverse material and personalities and needs that had been the crucial aspect of his role at BP. He also became for many years Chairman of the COI Branch of the Institute of Professional Civil Servants aka the Civil Service Union, requiring the same skills and self-effacing charm. He commuted daily to London from Wateringbury, Kent. We kids used to run down the hill with him, through the hop fields, to the station – Dad clutching a piece of toast, with his hair flying, and us kids with our satchels bumping on our backs. We often only caught the train by a whisker, the guard leaning out from the van shouting: "Come on, Mr. Webster! Take it at the back! Take it at the back!"   Even after my parents moved to Gloucestershire in 1960/1, while I was at university, Dad continued to commute to London, staying in digs with a landlady in Lewisham during the week. He didn't retire till he was seventy, and as his boss said then: "It is impossible to conceive of Neil being retired!"

## A security interlude

When in the post-War years of détente, the 1961 British Trade Fair in Moscow was organised, Dad was nominated to go in the COI delegation that would staff the British Exhibit. He asked for security clearance, since he had been employed on secret work at BP, and was given the OK. All went well, the delegate group made many friends, and Dad acquired a Russian music-buff pen pal. Not long afterwards, he began receiving invitations to functions – cocktail parties – at various minor Soviet bloc embassies. This caused him some anxiety. He repeatedly approached the security people for clearance and was always told to "Go ahead, old chap. Good for trade!" I was then a post-graduate studying in London and was sometimes asked by Dad to accompany him, suitably attired (not easy for a student) both to cheer me up and to provide him an invited 'guest'. On one occasion, he glanced round the room when we arrived at all the shining crowd, and recognised one or two, then three who each looked as uncomfortable as I felt. They were all ex BP. We left, and he declined any further invitations.

## The story breaks

In 1969-72, by coincidence I was living near Bletchley, working for the beginning Open University, when my husband was involved in early Milton Keynes. I could revisit childhood haunts in Fenny, but we never visited BP – even then little was known about the work there and the Park had not yet been saved for posterity. Dad did however arrange for us to meet Peter Calvocoressi, who still lived nearby. When the story of BP began to break in the mid 1970s, all of us in the family were very interested. I recall that on a US trip I acquired a copy of a book released in the US before the UK and took it home. He himself followed the developments closely, and after he retired in 1976 began working on his own book about his intelligence work, feeling that existing books so far were short on important elements.

Among Dad's papers is a draft preface written in early 1980 explaining clearly why he thought his version of the story should be told at that time. "It was my job to see that wireless intelligence gave the cryptographers all possible help in finding cribs... this aspect has hardly been mentioned in accounts so far ... Yet Bletchley's rapid and regular breaking [of Enigma], a major factor in Allied victory, was based on cribs, and accounts which omit this are simply 'Hamlet without the prince'." Added later in longhand notes is "Calvocoressi's account (1980) is inaccurate and Welchman's (1982), light on re-encodement".

By September1980, he had obtained formal written permission from GCHQ to publish his draft text, and then began working on the book in earnest. He sent copies of his draft to various BP colleagues, particularly Ronald Lewin and Ralph Bennett. He was then approached by Robin Denniston, the publisher at Oxford University Press. He was also corresponding with Jean Howard (of Hut 3) who in a letter refers to him as 'Neil Webster who was the person with the most substantial recollections of Y' (radio signals intelligence) and describes his draft text sent on to her as 'full of absolute gems'. They met up: Jean had been asked by Roy Davies of BBC TV to help with a planned programme commemorating D Day and she sent Dad a draft paper, and put him in touch with Roy Davies. All was going well when in August 1985 he learned that his permission to publish had been withdrawn, at the top level of GCHQ.

Shocked and upset, Dad consulted his solicitor and discussed the problem. From the correspondence one can see that his first reaction was to go ahead and publish anyway. He wrote formally to protest. On August 9, with many apologies GCHQ wrote that the original clearance decision had been wrong and that no amount of editing would get his draft into a form that GCHQ would consider fit for publication. Eventually wisdom and his long loyalty prevailed. He wrote: "Thank you for your apologies and the kindly way in which you informed me of your harsh decision. It amazes me that after all that has been published about breaking Enigma and after all the electronic and other technical developments of the past forty years, my little account of practical co-operation with Hut 6 is proscribed as of value to Britain's enemies. Of course I am bound to accept your ruling..." A deal was then arranged, of a cash payment to cover his expenses and disappointment and loss of face with his publisher. He also offered, voluntarily, to assign copyright in the text to GCHQ, which they gratefully accepted. I believe now that he did this because he was distressed to be in any way seen as a 'goose that cackled' after his long, loyal silence, and when he had very good reasons for wanting to break that silence.

In the following years, he was approached by some less scrupulous interested parties, and always turned them aside. In 1990 my father died.

Later, in the mid 1990s, my mother was approached by would-be exploiters of Dad's BP connection. But she informed GCHQ and was thanked for her action with: "You play a straight bat, Mrs Webster!" In 2007 my mother died, leaving the old house in Gloucestershire, and all its contents to her three surviving children, with me as an executor.

My two brothers and I had each followed the BP revelations and wondered what to do about Dad's book. In his filing cabinet (yes, the same war-issue cabinet I saw in childhood) we found draft MSs, a copy of the typescript of the whole book as it stood in 1985 when work ceased, and a clutch of correspondence - with his solicitor and GCHQ, and with colleagues and BP contacts. Godfrey (younger brother) had carried this all off to study, when in 2008 I received a letter forwarded by one of my mother's publishers, from a James Thirsk. Jimmy wrote to 'Dear Webster children' with condolences about my mother's death, and to tell us of the publication of his own book: *Bletchley Park: An Inmate's Story*, for which my mother had contributed many details about Dad. It seemed that she had still kept her silence about Dad's own book, as Jimmy when I later told him of it expressed surprise and knew only the official account written by my Dad with Alfred Sugar in 1946. Jimmy sent a copy of his own book, which is a very lively account with some great stories about the brilliant eccentrics of Beaumanor and BP, including about my Dad - his recruitment, his lateral thinking role in the Fusion Room, his affectionate nickname 'Wee Willie', his background and later life. Jimmy and I corresponded by email, and I began to feel it was about time to do something at last about Dad's book. He had a right to be heard, and his wartime contribution honoured.

It was at about this time that GCHQ released a mass of wartime records of BP to the National Archive at Kew. However when I began looking at them, there was one document that was restricted (and is still now in 2011) and 'retained by the department' - *The SIXTA History*. Since this was Dad's role – liaison between traffic analysis (SIXTA) and the cryptographers, I feared we would have no luck getting his book cleared. My elder brother Andrew then forwarded to me an account of SIXTA which was written by one of the Americans attached to BP – Robert Nunn – and was available on the web, with the comment that they were less sensitive about SIXTA in the US! It was then that Jimmy suggested that I simply write and ask for clearance.

In early December 2009 I followed his suggestion and wrote to GCHQ asking for permission for *Cribs for Victory* to be published. They replied, apologizing that despite an extensive archive search, they could not find the manuscript but nonetheless regretfully felt that the correspondence made it clear that permission was unlikely to be granted 'because of the continuing sensitivity around much of the history of SIXTA...'. They also asked if the family themselves had a copy of the manuscript as their Departmental Historian would very much like to see it. I then sent them a photocopy of the only extant TS. Following communication with me on various matters, in April everything changed. They wrote charmingly giving permission for publication at last and offering, of their own volition, to issue a copyright license to enable this, though still retaining the copyright themselves. In July the draft license arrived. It gave us permission to publish without any charge to ourselves or our eventual publisher, leaving us free to prepare the book for publication.

To find a publisher, I contacted Jerry Johns of the Polperro Heritage Press. He had published *Thirty Secret Years* by Robin Denniston, the man with whom my father had been in discussion at OUP, now retired. Jerry quickly stepped in, and became our publisher. He has done much to help us in preparing the book. Sections have been added, notably my father's war letters, plus biographical material, correspondence in the 1980s with BP colleagues, research on 'Fusion to SIXTA', and a glossary.

### Reasons why

It is only natural that the family should wonder why permission to publish was withdrawn and then held back for so long. Why was there, and is there now, 'continuing sensitivity around the history of SIXTA'? We have speculated that my father, being innocent of 'side' and unaware of jealousies, trod on a few toes in his book (see particularly 'Contributions to Intelligence'). Again, as Dad himself was aware, Welchman's book, *The Hut 6 Story*, and indeed his subsequent more exposing papers about BP, caused a lot of upset, not only in the US but also in GCHQ. In his book *Enigma*, Hugh Sebag Montefiore relates how in August 1985, the then GCHQ Director wrote a furious letter to Welchman. It was a few days later that he rescinded Dad's permission to publish.

But, for my money, I believe that *Cribs for Victory* is too close to the real truth about how Enigma was broken, and the inner workings of British intelligence. Reading the paper written in 1984 by Jean Howard, included here, one can see that at this time SIXTA and the Fusion Room were still controversial and clouded in the confusion caused by conflicting departmental memories.

Dad's book is just too clear, both about the relationship between signals intelligence and cryptography, and about the habits of the German military mind that opened the door to understanding Enigma.

# Part I

## ABOUT *CRIBS FOR VICTORY*

The book is just as Neil left it in 1985. Whether he would have extended or adapted it, in the light of later books, we don't know. But reading it now, I think it stands the test of time well. It is fresh, sharp, fast-paced and precisely informative and as he promises in his introduction, "not too solemn". As one of his colleagues said of him, "Neil has a nice sense of the absurd!" The middle of the book is densely technical – as it has to be to elucidate the challenges tackled by my father and his colleagues, to understand both signals intelligence (SIGINT) and the needs of cryptographers, and their interwoven and continuing feedback on crucial wartime intelligence. The book also has a serious message. Its central argument is that traffic analysis and cryptography - the twin faces of intelligence – should be integrated in a single discipline. Most of all it conveys the comradeship and spirit of the chase - the hunt for cribs, the failures and the rewards: "After all," he says, "we were digging for gold!"

# Cribs for Victory

## Neil Webster

# INTRODUCTION

In 1940 a little band of amiable and unworldly academics, hired by a small secret department of the Foreign Office, walked unconcernedly through red tape, short-circuited official and military channels, planned an inter-service organisation to produce intelligence on a conveyor belt, and got it established in spite of some initial resistance by the separate armed services. For the rest of World War II this intelligence factory controlled the interception of enemy radio communications, broke most of the great bulk of secret enciphered messages intercepted, and passed on their contents - translated, annotated and with their source carefully disguised - to Churchill and the concerned commands usually within a few hours and sometimes within a few minutes of their interception.

This flow of intelligence had profound effects. In the Battle of Britain the decodes gave the German bombing targets and indications of their overall strategy and true losses. In Africa they gave details of Rommel's plans and dispositions. In the critical Battle of the Atlantic, they turned the tide by pinpointing submarine packs. Of their use on the Second Front Eisenhower wrote that they had simplified his task enormously, saved thousands of British and American lives and speeded up the rout of the enemy. The total influence of the decodes is, however, hard to gauge. Cryptography and radio intelligence were so interlinked and interdependent, that it is not sensible to try to evaluate their contributions separately. Together, besides directly affecting strategic and tactical decisions, they provided a solid framework of knowledge on which the planning and evaluation of other intelligence operations could be based. These operations e.g. reconnaissance and espionage also acted as a cover for the cryptographic success. The Germans never tumbled to the fact that their main cipher, Enigma machine cipher, was regularly and promptly broken.

This is the extraordinary story of Station X, the Government Code and Cipher School at Bletchley Park in Buckinghamshire. Equally extraordinary is the fact that this story was kept not only from the enemy in war time but from the whole of the world's press for twenty five years after the war's end. Stranger still perhaps is the fact that Bletchley Park's success was based on the exploitation of those very qualities of tidiness and systematic order which were the virtues of the German military mind.

The German armed forces had prepared meticulously for their drive to conquer the world. They had taken over the concept of the blitzkrieg, the lightning breakthrough spearheaded by massed tanks, which had been advocated by Liddell-Hart and other British military strategists, but decisively rejected by the British military establishment. The Germans had developed this concept to include close air support by dive bombers and co-ordination of operations by a comprehensive radio network linking formations at all levels. Command cars had a radio and radio operator on board and were allocated one or two frequencies in the 3000-8000 kHz band to communicate with their subordinate units. Such communication was independent of land-line interruption and could be maintained while moving. It was swift, orderly and disciplined.

To prevent the enemy picking up their dispositions and plans by listening to their traffic, they devised a system of daily changing call signs for station recognition and sought and, they thought, found the perfect cipher combining speed and simplicity of operation with absolute security. This was Enigma machine cipher. So in a German command car besides the radio there was also a call sign book and an Enigma cipher machine together with instructions for the daily change of call signs and cipher machine settings.

A cipher used by units engaged in active fighting cannot base its security on the assumption that its general system will not become known to the enemy or that a cipher machine, if one is used, will not fall into enemy hands. Even in this last case it must be impossible for the enemy to find out the setting for the day and decipher the messages. The German high command thought this to be true of Enigma machine cipher and it was not unreasonable of them to think so. The machine was capable of forty million million million different settings. So what went wrong with their calculations? Well, the perfect machine cipher must be proof not only against capture or reconstruction of the machine but against the enemy's ability to guess part of the contents of certain messages and to deduce from this the machine setting for the day. Enigma machine cipher proved vulnerable to this approach owing to certain features of the cipher itself, the brilliance of Polish and British cryptographers and the German love of order and pattern which made guessing much easier.

The Poles worked out the basic principles for breaking Enigma machine cipher from 'cribs' (messages whose clear text could be guessed) and handed over what they knew to the British just before Poland was over-run. The British developed at Bletchley Park the organisation, methods and machinery to exploit these principles to the full. In particular, they developed a new approach based on the marriage of cryptography and radio intelligence and involving close co-operation between cryptographers and the Y Service, i.e. the intercept stations and parties responsible for the study of the German radio networks. This key aspect of the complex Bletchley Park operation has not been dealt with adequately in the accounts published so far. So, as I became the Major on liaison between the central Y service party at Bletchley and the cryptographers, it seems to me worthwhile to give a brief account of who we were and what we did.

Who we were - what sort of people we were, how and why recruited, how we lived, our relations with our colleagues, our families and the 'locals' - has seemed to me an important part of the story and one which would be misrepresented if told too solemnly.

# THE LONDON SCOTTISH

Some people, even in 1940, got into signals intelligence by relatively orthodox routes, i.e. through signals units and the course at Matlock. But there were other ways, various and sometimes curious. Neither job seekers nor recruiters lacked enterprise and imagination.

I myself got in through a combination of my own laziness and curiosity and the loyalty and sheer gall of my comrades in arms. So I suppose I started unknowingly on the road to Bletchley Park in May, 1939, when I joined the newly forming 298 Battery, third battalion the London Scottish. My father, a retired Indian Civil Servant and a patriot, suggested this; and I agreed, though not for his reasons. I did not particularly want to die defending a class-ridden and backward-looking Britain, living complacently on cheap food and raw materials from poor countries.  But I did want to stop the advance of German militarism. I hated the arrogance and underlying cruelty of the young Nazis I met in London, the calm assumption that we could not resist them and must join them. 'After all, you are Anglo-Saxon, part of the  Herren Volk.  Come with us and we will divide the world.'

'Oh no!' I would murmur. 'You're mistaken. The British are the lost tribes of Israel'.  So I joined the Scottish, a tiny ridiculous gesture of defiance.

The battery was at annual camp at Aberporth in Wales, when war broke out; and came straight back to Kent to dig emplacements and man anti-aircraft guns. We were an extraordinary unit, a collection of strange and powerful characters: actors, writers, musicians, advertising men, lawyers, managers, entrepreneurs and professional gamblers and desperados. Ernie Marples, later Minister of Transport and a peer, was our quartermaster sergeant. He got the job after being confined to barracks for breaking camp to visit his newly wed wife. To redeem himself, he then wrote to the colonel, pointing out that the stores were in a dreadful mess and that only he, Marples, could put things straight. George Salmon of the family that owned Lyons tea shops was our catering corporal. He recruited good Lyons cooks for us. At night I would hear him turning restlessly and muttering in his sleep 'Cocoa! Cocoa! They must have cocoa!' - real Jewish inner drive and devotion to the job in hand.

Our camp concerts had a professional polish with sketches and songs by Paul Dehn, Gilbert Armitage, Alan McKinnon (script writer of *This Man Is News*), and Nigel Burgess, an old Etonian advertising man with whom I struck up a friendship. Nigel was later to become an MI5 major and ironically had to keep an eye on communism in the trade unions, though his brother Guy was in fact already a Russian agent and was later to defect to Russia.

There were in the battery several men who had fought in the Spanish civil war. One told me he had become a colonel but 'so did anyone with a good pair of long boots!' Of course, there was a Bonham Carter while at the other end of the social scale was a meths-drinking Irishman called Skelly, a barrack room lawyer, who knew Kings Regulations backwards and yet spent most of his time in the guard room, where he fascinated his guards with his consummate skill in telling a never ending stream of stories of Irish love, cunning and magic.

At the beginning of 1940 a group of Scottish immatures joined the battery. They were tough, foul-mouthed, proud, touchy, romantic little teen-age volunteers from the Glasgow slums. And we got on very well with them. A month later conscripted men began to appear and they, at any rate at first, were harder to assimilate. The immatures could not stand them. They found them soft, sissy and self-regarding. In fact the conscripts were largely ordinary working class lads leaving home for the first time and must have found us all rather strange and frightening.

In March 1940 the original enlisted men began to leave rapidly to officer training units or directly to commissions. The battery wanted to place me too, but had never known what to do with me. I was small and slight, untidy, clumsy, impractical and absent-minded; and not at all dominant or aggressive by London Scottish standards. So I was unsuited to command men in action, while I had no obvious special qualifications. I had reached the age of 33 without ever holding a salaried post and, after bumming around the States, had been coasting along on a small private income, trying to set myself up as a literary agent.

At first, in September 1939, I was sent to Battalion headquarters at Wickham Court (a commandeered luxury hotel) as cookhouse orderly and sergeants' mess waiter - a month of hell, fortunately interrupted by a blissful and hilarious 48 hour marriage leave.

Fearing the battery's posting abroad, my child-faced but very determined bride had persuaded the ecclesiastical authorities to grant a special licence and we were married on 13th September at St. Gabriels, Warwick Square, Pimlico. I was in civvies as my battledress was too big for me. The ring stuck but fortunately went on after the best man, my brother Patrick, whispered 'Lick it, you fool!' We had a wedding lunch without a wedding cake or the bride's mother at the Rubens Hotel in Buckingham Palace Road, while a German-Jewish gentleman, a friendly alien waiting to be interned, hung conspicuously around outside, because he did not want to compromise a serving soldier by coming in. My mother had for some reason booked us in at the Wellington Hotel in Tunbridge Wells. It proved to have large cold dismal bedrooms named after naval battles and a clientele of crabbed old residents who became furiously jealous, when a table lamp with a pink shade was placed on the honeymooners' table. Table lamps for every table had to be brought by a procession of waitresses. We fled in the morning to the chromium and gilt comfort of the Selsdon Park Hotel, the as yet un-commandeered sister hotel of Wickham Court, where we drank champagne in the bath and from which an old chauffeur-driven Rolls returned me to Wickham Court and the Augean task of cleaning cellars whose crumbly brick floors were a foot deep in sodden paper hats and streamers and other wastes of pleasure.

In November after a battalion dance to which I brought my lovely bride, I was posted back to the battery and put on telescopes - a pleasant task for which however I was totally unsuited. Not that my eyesight was poor - I had been passed for commercial flying in the States. But I was just not a spotter. As a child, I always lost out at hunt-the-thimble. And the battery knew it. 'He wouldn't spot the Queen Mary,' they said, 'if she came between number one and number two gun sites!' However I did manage to devise a simple quick calculator for aiming corrections, which impressed my friends.

For a time I tried to prepare for liaison with the French. I read a French gunnery manual and an extraordinary British manual on tactics, which noted the Germans' use of tanks for break-through in their manoeuvres and wrote it off as a publicity stunt and quite impractical in real war.

The decision on what finally to do with me was reached in April 1940. It happened like this. 'How would you like to get off fatigues?' Nigel Burgess asked me as we were going on parade at Dartford. 'Yes,' I answered, largely out of curiosity. 'Well,' said Nigel, 'when they say 'Fall out special fatigues', fall out with me and we'll do the leave cards and ration allowances!' So we did. But Nigel left me in the lurch and there was a scrummage and a riot, after which an officer came asking 'Why can't Webster do a simple job like that?' Nigel Burgess and Alan McKinnon rallied to my aid. 'Webster has a great brain' said Nigel 'He should not be here at all. He should be in the War Office.' 'But what could he do?' said the officer, scratching his head. Alan delved in his fertile imagination. 'Codes and ciphers' he pronounced in his deep mysterious Scottish voice.

And sure enough in three weeks I was sent for interview at number 3 Caxton Street, having in the meantime boned up what I could from encyclopaedias about ciphers and their breaking. To my surprise, they took me.

## CAXTON STREET AND BOLITHO'S ANGELS

In May after the birth of my first child Andrew Peter I reported in my ill-fitting gunner's battledress to Colonel Stratton at No 3 Caxton Street, but was told by him that he was expecting a Lieutenant Webster and that I had better go out and buy myself a uniform. So I did and pranced through the streets with my swagger cane, though in fact he was wrong. I was not gazetted for another two weeks. This was not quite fair on the other two recruits, who were to be gazetted about the same time but for some reason had not been told to put up a pip at once. These two were Chris Wills and Hamish Blair Cunynghame, who were to work close to me for much of the war. Soon, however, we were all three second lieutenants and formed a unit assisted by a sergeant and a rogue of a corporal acting as a clerk.

I was the oldest and started out as head of the unit, but I could not manage the rogue corporal and relinquished the headship to the tall dynamic Hamish, who was good at bullying and cajoling difficult and stupid people.

We had not, I soon realized, joined the cryptographers but number 6 Intelligence School, which was being set up by MI8 to study the enemy communications systems. Our primary task, we were given to understand by Stratton, was to break the call sign system used by the German air force. However Stratton's explanation both of this task and of the organisation to accomplish it, was pretty vague and inadequate. A tubby little professor of astronomy, he longed to be back in his observatory and his heart was not in wireless intelligence. So we had to take our own bearings and only gradually did we begin to understand the complexities.

What was immediately apparent was that our floor was inhabited by some two dozen civilian women of very Mayfair style, who spent their time recording on punched cards the call signs and frequencies used by the German armed forces. These women, I discovered, had been recruited in rather a strange way. A certain Captain Bolitho had made something of a name for himself in wireless intelligence by inventing a device for 'finger printing' the bleeps of transmitters. Somehow he got the War Office to agree to his recruiting his own band of bright, well-connected women and using them on top secret work. Mary, the first he recruited, described to me how it happened. Her sister was at a wedding early in 1940, when a man asked if she wanted a job. She didn't, she had one. 'Pity! My brother wants a smart girl'. But when she got home, she told Mary and after various ringings up, a man's voice came on the phone.

'Are you Mary?' 'Yes'

'Do you want a job?' 'Yes'

'Meet me outside the Ritz at 6.30' 'How shall I know you?' 'I'm six foot five!' So Mary went and got the job. Later she brought a friend for Bolitho to look at. He did just that, he sat silently looking at the girls and sucking his pipe.

Finally Mary burst out laughing.

'Well, does she get the job?

'Of course she gets the job. Come and have a glass of champagne'.

Mary told this like something out of Evelyn Waugh, but in fact Bolitho's recruitment methods were highly successful. He got a marvellous bunch. Later we recruited direct from the universities and used intelligence and aptitude test but these later recruits were not on average up to 'Bolitho's Angels'. He was probably checking up through the social network, which at this level tends to be franker and more demanding than teachers and employers. Three of his recruits in particular - Judith Whitfield, Elizabeth Roscoe and Iva Dundas - were to become key personnel, vital to the organisation of our work.

Bolitho did not pay his recruits out of his own pocket, though he did buy the punched card machines and other office equipment. The women he simply told that if they were prepared to start working for nothing, the government would be paying them within three months. He was right. By the time I arrived, they were all civil servants. Bolitho himself was not now working with this part of the organisation. But he was living in the St Ermins Hotel, which formed part of the same block as number 3 Caxton Street and was connected to it by a passage. His huge, loose figure would appear sometimes at night, when we had to keep some kind of watch. And if there was nothing on, he might invite some of us to his flat in the St Ermins to see 'some pictures of cows', i.e. films of his Argentinian hacienda.

By day Bolitho would visit the office and wander around, prodding the punched card machine and other office equipment and furniture and saying 'Do you know whose these are? They're mine and I haven't been paid for them'.

Pretty soon however, all this was settled and we then saw little more of this kindly and surprising man, who lent me his car when my wife came up to London for a brief spree and who maintained the little flower bed under the Admiralty Arch, which I had always thought was publicly maintained.

Besides our unit and Bolitho's angels there was on our floor a Captain Wishart, a statistician, who was presumably supposed to organise research into the German system of call sign allocation, while on the floor above there were other officers including Major Tozer and Lieutenant (soon Captain)

Crankshaw. We did not at first know the nature of the upstairs work, but were later told that they were studying the German armed forces radio network in the light of decodes of German messages. We also came to know that a party under Captain Lithgow was doing similar work at a mysterious place known variously as Station X, BP, Bletchley Park or Bletchley, where the German ciphers, including the machine cipher called Enigma, were broken. It was impressed on us that Bletchley's cryptographic success was a secret of the highest importance, which the civilians and other ranks on our floor were not supposed to share.

The upstairs party was soon joined by a new recruit - Freddie Edwards. Freddie was a tall powerfully built young blond, whose eyesight was so bad that everything more than two feet away was a blur and he could read only by holding a book opposite his ear and reading out of the corner of his eye. So he had been graded very logically as unfit for active service and put in the pioneer corps to dig trenches. What had not been taken into account, was that he had been a boy chess champion and had learned to read from chess textbooks and that his German was pretty good.

Freddie had heard that there was some sort of interesting place at number 3 Caxton Street. So he went there carrying a plain official envelope marked 'Captain Smith, to be delivered personally'. Fortune was with him. The answer came back. 'Captain Smith is out, but Major Tozer will see you'. After talking to Freddie, Tozer said, 'The body stays. The transfer comes through later'. I think Freddie came originally as a private, but he was soon a sergeant and ended the war as a captain.

In the meantime Hamish, Chris and I had set about trying to help solve the German call sign system from the sources available to us. To understand what these were requires some explanation both of the German armed forces' systems of radio communication and of the procedures and records used at the British intercept stations eavesdropping on them.

The radio communications of the German armed forces were on a huge scale and, to avoid confusion, were based on the star system, whereby all communication was to, from or through the control of the 'star'. Control had no call sign. It called an outstation by using the same call sign, which that outstation used to call control. Usually each star was allocated one or two frequencies and these frequencies would stay the same for long periods. The frequency was thus an important factor in identifying a 'star' picked up by our interceptors, and my memory for numbers proved useful; but it was seldom enough in itself for reliable identification of the 'star' and did not identify the individual station. Call signs of course existed to do just that if the system of call sign allocation was known. But the call signs, which consisted of three symbols (either letters or numbers), changed daily according to a system, which we had not solved.

The communications between the stations on the German 'stars' were in Morse code and consisted of message transmissions, most of which were in cipher or code (usually machine cipher from regiment or *staffel* upwards), and operators chat (keying, calling, notice and receipt of messages, queries, checks, cancellations etc.) which was mainly in the international Q code used for brevity, not security, by most Morse senders throughout the world. The British operators monitoring these communications at the intercept stations set up for this purpose at Chatham (later moved to Woodhouse near Loughborough), Chicksands, Harpenden, and elsewhere, had to hunt around the frequency bands to find transmissions of the German armed forces or to listen on frequencies where they expected to find particular 'stars'; and to make two types of record of what they heard. First of all, they had to write down every message on a message pad and, as soon as it was completed, hand it over for despatch to the cryptographers at Bletchley. Secondly they had to record all operators chat and the preambles of messages in a log or, as the Americans called it perhaps more aptly, a chatter sheet. The logs were handed over to intelligence officers at the intercept station who compiled from them a daily report of the frequencies and call signs of the 'stars' heard. These reports were sent to 3 Caxton Street (among other places) and formed the basis of the attempted analysis of the call sign system.

The call-sign book used by the German army had been captured. It contained 40,000 three-symbol call signs arranged in 200 columns by 200 rows. Military stars were allocated a column for the day, while their stations were each allocated one or more rows, which they kept while the column changed daily. The system of column allocation had not yet been solved but it was believed to be some kind of grid applied to a reordering of the columns.

Interest in the German Army's communications, however, was low in the summer of 1940. The fighting in Europe was over. The Battle of Britain was on. The air force call-sign system was the thing. We suspected that it was similar to the army system, but the evidence was confusing and conflicting. We changed from punched card recording to manual indexing, which we thought might throw up leads during the actual process of writing on the card. Elizabeth Roscoe and I compiled a large chart, which should have shown the reappearance together of call signs from the same column of the supposed call sign book. But the evidence was inconclusive and we gave up.

I was, I think, chicken-hearted. There was some positive evidence and the inconsistencies were due to the unreliability of the material. The intercept operators were brilliant at finding German air force traffic and picking out the 'stars' they were meant to be covering but even so they tended to pick up and confuse call signs of separate stars on neighbouring frequencies and to make errors in recording transmissions difficult to hear, while the recorded frequencies for the same star might for a variety of reasons vary from day to day. The intelligence officers at the intercept stations, whose primary concern was to see that they gave Bletchley the messages it wanted, had little time to sort out these matters when making their daily reports.

One reason for my giving up so easily was that we had begun to adopt a new short-term approach to the problem of star and station recognition. We were now receiving some of the actual logs from the intercept stations. And we had begun to set some of the staff to 'log reading' i.e. to summarising from the logs the pattern of communication of a 'star' by means of a diagram with arrows showing the direction of messages, a list of message preambles and notes of significant chat. These summaries, it was found, made it possible to recognise stars and some of the stations on them from day to day even without knowing the call sign system. Crankshaw was fascinated by the diagrams. For when taken together with the addresses, signatures and operating instructions supplied to him from the decodes they helped him to build up a picture in depth of the German air force chain of communication, which was in effect the chain of command, i.e. the order of battle. Elizabeth Roscoe, who was nearly always right, pointed out that the improved identifications provided by log reading might make it easier to reconstruct the call sign system, but by that time I was more interested in short-term results.

The effort put into log reading was accordingly increased. New staff, largely ATS, were recruited and the log reading party was moved out of the London blitz to the Warren, a large house at Harpenden and put under the command of Crankshaw, now a captain. A small party was left behind in London to try to work out the air force call sign system, which they did successfully about two years later. A little earlier Malcolm Spooner working on his own at the intercept station at Beaumanor solved the similar system by which the German army allocated the columns from their similar but separate call sign book. Eventually a copy of the actual call sign book used by the German air force was captured and almost at the same time the Russians gave us a second captured copy.

# HARPENDEN AND BEAUMANOR

I was glad to be out of London. My room in Pimlico had been pretty terrifying in the blitz and I had spent many nights in the basement at Dolphin Square. Fortunately I left before the million to one chance bomb came through the narrow ventilator shaft and killed everyone in that basement.

In Harpenden I soon managed to find a terribly suburban furnished house to which I brought my wife and baby. We stayed there till the following summer, when the unit moved to Beaumanor, a manor house at Woodhouse between Loughborough and Leicester. After three months living in Beaumanor, I got an idyllic furnished cottage on the outskirts of the neighbouring village of Woodhouse Eaves owing to the kindness of Judith Whitfield, Elizabeth Roscoe and Iva Dundas, who had found it for themselves but gave it up for the sake of my baby and my pregnant wife. Woodhouse Eaves turned out to be the country seat of a branch of my wife's family, the Heygates. My daughter was born there and my family stayed there happily till the spring of 1943 when they moved temporarily back to my parents' home in Cheltenham. I myself moved to Bletchley with the unit in the summer of 1942, but managed to visit my family fairly often both at Woodhouse Eaves and in Cheltenham.

The story of the work at Harpenden and Beaumanor is essentially one of expansion, increasing knowledge of German armed forces communications and improving methods of analysis and quality of work. The organisation of the unit was and continued from now on to be in two main parts - the log readers and the relatively small fusion room in which the log readers' summaries were put together with information from decodes. We became experienced in identifying 'stars' and their stations from a combination of indications - frequency, number of stations, type of traffic or chat, working routine - quite apart from the content of decodes. Direction finding too, though not of great precision on high frequencies at long range, could be useful in deciding between alternative identifications or in indicating large movements. The practical results of our work, however, were limited by our physical separation from Bletchley Park, our lack of knowledge of its needs and its lack of knowledge of what we had to offer.

The first thing that Crankshaw did when we got to Harpenden was to call the log readers together and on his own initiative let them into the secret that Enigma, the German machine cipher, was being broken. Tozer was angry with Crankshaw about this, but said pragmatically, 'Well, it's done!' Crankshaw told me that he felt he had to do this. He just could not work with people who did not know in broad outline what he was doing. There was however still much ambivalence about the security position. Even those who had been told knew little or nothing about the nature of the Enigma cipher, the methods used for breaking it, the extent of present success or the contribution which their own work might make to such success. Moreover new recruits to the unit were not told anything. This was as well as not every face fitted and some moved on. For instance, Aubrey Jones and a friend of his were posted to Harpenden, took an instant dislike to the unit, refused to talk to anyone and walked about the garden at the Warren like a pair of Italian carabinieri. They moved on within a week.

On our move to Beaumanor, Crankshaw left us, first, I think, for Bletchley and then to join the British Military Mission to Russia. Hamish Blair Cunynghame, who was already in charge of the log reading operation, took over general charge of the unit's work, though a regular officer, Colonel Thompson, was for a time put in over his head. This led to some conflict. Thompson wanted to make the unit more military and keep it separate from Bletchley. But Hamish got his way. He visited Bletchley and talked with Gordon Welchman and Stuart Milner-Barry, the top men of Hut 6, which was responsible for breaking German army and air force Enigma messages. Welchman and Milner-Barry came down to Beaumanor, looked around and arranged for some of their cryptographers to spend some weeks with us as log readers. These scouts reported back that they had learned much which was useful to them and which explained things that had puzzled them; and they praised the quality and value of the work at Beaumanor, which few people at Bletchley appreciated. Moreover they felt that the security situation was a bit vague and anomalous and that it would be much better from this point of view too if the unit was moved to work within the Bletchley Park perimeter and was properly inducted into the Ultra secret. Welchman and Milner-Barry concurred; Welchman in particular had an instinct that our move to Bletchley would prove important.

In the summer of 1942 we accordingly moved to Bletchley and absorbed Lithgow's party, the small radio intelligence party already at Bletchley and engaged in building up the communications picture from decodes. Lithgow himself moved to London to play his part in the radio intelligence operation against the Japanese.

I do not want to give the impression that our work at Harpenden and Beaumanor was valuable only as a preparation for our work at Bletchley. We did build up the communications picture; we did supply some leads to the cryptographers; and we did help to provide indications of major new strategic intentions such as the German abandonment of the invasion of Britain, their offensives against Russia and the Balkans, and the start of Rommel's North African campaign, and in two instances at least we made contributions of great importance.

The first was in regard to the German signals regiment associated with navigational beams for bombers and experimental work on advanced weapons, such as flying bombs, rockets and atomic bombs. The radio operators on this 'star' were expert technicians with a very high speed of Morse operation and a contempt for ordinary security. They passed to each other Enigma messages in their own series of Enigma settings and an extraordinary jumble of Q code, their own improvised codes and abbreviations and even *en clair*. Hut 6 had broken some days of their Enigma messages and the decodes were being studied by Professor Norman, the bouncy little professor with the jaunty walk and twirling walking stick. He found the decodes by themselves rather puzzling, but when he put them together with our log readers' summaries of the total communication on the star, he began to grasp what was going on, to work out the significance of all the chat and thus substantially to supplement and interpret the decodes. Sometimes too he found leads, e.g. the revelation in chat of part of the cipher setting, which led to further Enigma breaks. All this was a substantial log reader contribution in an important area and started when we were at Harpenden.

The other vital contribution was made when we were at Beaumanor and may well have affected the whole course of the war.

Enigma messages were sent in five letter groups. The first five letter group was from mid-1940 until 1944 a dummy group, the last three letters of which served as an indication of the setting which was being used. There were different settings every day and on each day for different groups and purposes. Each setting could be recognised by the use of any one of four different combinations of three letters allocated to it. These three letter labels were known to us as discriminants.

The intercept station operator included the dummy first group in the message preambles, which he put on the log. So the log readers in their summaries could distinguish different Enigma settings. For working purposes we referred to the different keys, i.e. the different series of daily settings for different groups and purposes, by codenames, largely the names of colours.

In 1940 the main keys were Red (the main air force key, the *Luftwaffe-maschinen-schlussel*; Violet (the air force administrative key, the *luftgaumaschinenschlussel*) and Brown (the key of the experimental signals regiment). There was also a practice key, which we called 'Blue'.

Just before Rommel started his attack in Africa, new army keys began to appear, but it was some time before Hut 6 managed to break them and in the meantime Rommel had pushed forward and was rolling up the British army. In addition to the army keys there appeared an army-air force liaison key (*fliegerverbin dungschlussel*) which we called Scorpion and separate air force and air force administrative keys for the area, which we called Light Blue and Primrose.

At Beaumanor we decided to put one of our junior officers, a certain Rodney Bax (later a judge), to do research on the pattern of discriminants. He sat in an old fashioned bathroom on the wide lid of the ancient private seat while his assistants including Staff Sergeant Sugar (later publicity officer of the Co-operative Union) worked on a board put over the bath. After some weeks of fruitless research, he came upon the interesting fact that the current Scorpion was repeating the Primrose discriminants of a couple of months ago in a scrambled order of days. Blair Cunynghame told Hut 6, who promptly checked. Yes, Scorpion was repeating the old Primrose settings, which had all been broken. The settings were cabled to Cairo, which could now intercept and read Scorpion at once without the delays caused by the need to break and the overburdened top secret communication links with England. It could not have been more opportune. It was just before Rommel's final push towards Cairo and the main contents of Scorpion consisted of orders to bomber unit (sent to army units for information) and position reports on the German front line (so that the air force should not bomb its own troops). I was told that when the Stukas (fourteen, I think) were sent in to soften up the British defences before the final ground attack, the Hurricanes were waiting for them and shot them all down.

# BLETCHLEY: THE SCENE

I moved to Bletchley in the summer of 1942 and became the lodger of a lady whose husband worked for the gas company. A kind, anxious woman with an anxious small boy, she fed me and looked after me well in her clean characterless semi-detached house with the linoleum floors. Then for a couple of months I moved to a very different home, a spotlessly scrubbed working class terrace house with a coal range, a copper and an outside lavatory. My new landlady was a big, formidable woman, wife of a railwayman and chairman of the local co-operative society. Her son, just graduated from Oxbridge, had got accepted for a job at the Park and was trying to persuade his parents to let him spend some of his salary on modernising their home. The clash of cultures became acute when the boy, returning hot and tired from a bike ride, forgot the routine of putting the plug in the bath before heating the copper and siphoned away all his bath water.

In the spring of 1944 I bought a small house in Fenny Stratford on the outskirts of Bletchley. My wife and three children joined me and we stayed there till the summer of 1946. We had good neighbours, the manager of the local brush factory, his wife and a fifteen year old daughter who was devoted to our children. My wife ran a little nursery school for our children and a few children of neighbours and friends from the Park.

Quite early in my contacts with the good people of Bletchley I learned about them a creditable and rather surprising fact. They never asked about our work. And so far as I could make out they did not gossip about it. They did however gossip endlessly in amazed tones about the strange ways and terrible morals of the people working at the Park.

This was not surprising. Bletchley was an old-fashioned small railway town with a very respectable working class and lower middle class population, while the people I found working in the Park were from quite a variety of very different worlds. In addition to a few career civil servants and soldiers they came from the universities and art colleges (sense of pattern and dexterity were important in some jobs), the professions, the artistic and literary worlds and the social worlds of Mayfair and Chelsea.

The civilians and many of the commissioned officers were in lodgings, flats or houses in Bletchley and the surrounding areas. Fleets of buses and estate cars brought the more distantly housed to and from work. A camp for military personnel both men and women was established at Shenley Road within short walking distance of the Park gates. I did a weeks tour of duty as duty officer at the camp. The American soldiers, who joined the Park in 1943 were in their own barracks apart from a few senior officers.

I myself walked or bicycled to work each day. The guards at the gate soon got to know me and did not need to look at my pass. I would walk past them, past the big house, past the lawns and the little lake with the Chinese geese to the huts and breeze block buildings where the work was done.

Like so much else at Bletchley, security was efficient without being fussy. Once one was inside the perimeter, there was no sense of being watched and no military bull. Bletchley had little interest in rank, but a great respect for personality and a great tolerance for eccentricity. I cannot confirm the story that someone for a bet walked about the Park in a white Prussian uniform for three days without attracting attention, but it is consistent with Bletchley's style. At the same time I think we were all sharply aware of the essential security rule; not a word about our work must be breathed outside the perimeter. And in this we had, as I have said, the co-operation of the people of Bletchley.

There was, however, one occasion, when the lyric of a comic song given at an entertainment in the hall just outside the perimeter was felt to come perilously near to indiscretion. Parodying the spiritual *Shadrak, Meshach and Abednigo*, Reg Parker wrote about the men who burned secret waste, 'We burn it - sec very sec, top sec, Phew!' It was the 'Phew!' that was felt by some to be close enough to the unmentionable top-sec U (Ultra) to cause gasps and raised eyebrows among the initiate and therefore curiosity among outsiders. However, I cannot believe that any harm was done.

We worked long hours at Bletchley Park but the work was absorbing and the place was full of talented, charming and approachable people and we did have time to meet for recreation and society as well as work. There was a marvellous chess club. Doctor Aitken, the Scottish champion, came regularly, while Golembek came occasionally. Alexander and Milner-Barry, the other top class players were usually too busy to come but there were many other good players. There was a fair amount of dramatic and musical talent prepared to put on play readings, plays, sketches and concerts. There were dances. There was conversation on the lawn by the lake with the Chinese geese.

Above all, however, there was the camaraderie and excitement of work. I was lucky in that my job as a liaison officer made it essential to roam around different huts and explore how I could help. Going into a Hut 6 research section I would sometimes find the girl cryptographers jumping for joy and shouting 'It's out! It's out!' when a new key was broken. Going into Hut 6 watch with its young men and women in bright coloured shirts and corduroy trousers and just a few British and American uniforms, I could sense the esprit de corps - alert, easy, warm and quite unmilitary .

It was this unmilitary atmosphere which was reported to have annoyed a visiting American general, who after being shown round Bletchley Park was asked if he had any questions, 'Well,' he is said to have said, 'I guess there is just one thing. Who in hell are these plush arse bastards?' He meant the Hut 6 watch in their corduroys. He cannot have understood much.

On the other hand, the American soldiers, officers and other ranks who joined us at Bletchley in 1942/3 had no such prejudices and fitted in splendidly. They decided not to wear their foreign service medals, while they were with us. They said they felt silly wearing them in front of civilians without medals, who had been in the London blitz. The American sergeants and corporals who joined our log reading unit were each allotted an experienced log reader, usually an ATS girl, to teach them and quickly won all hearts by their total lack of swank. They were mainly young graduates carefully selected for suitability for working with British back-room staff. American officers came into the Hut 6 and Hut 3 watches and American officers and other ranks into other parts of Hut 6. I got very friendly with some of them, particularly with tall ugly charming Bill Bijur, who brought his own brand of slightly Marx Brothers humour into our social life and our entertainment. With a casquette on his head and his chin pulled in he could look the spitting image of General de Gaulle. He did a wonderful production of *Yes, My Darling Daughter* with all the American parts played by the British and himself as a drawling stage Englishman. He died of cancer shortly after the war but I can still hear his voice greeting me cheerfully as I went into the Hut 6 watch ,'Hullo Neil. Still bumming?' Yes, of course I was 'bumming'. It was my job, liaison in official language. But to understand just why I was bumming, it is necessary to explain in broad outline the cryptographic position at Bletchley and the ways in which our unit could contribute to its work.

# THE CRYPTOGRAPHIC BACKGROUND

The German forces at all levels appeared to love logical systems. They were averse to the tedious and untidy process of putting names or numbers in a hat, shaking it and drawing at random. If they had a readymade formula or pattern to hand, they found it neat and economical to use it. But they would also think up systems and formulas.

This German characteristic was a help to radio intelligence. For instance, if number 1 *staffel* had call sign rows 1, 3 and 5, it was a good bet that number 2 *staffel* had 2, 4 and 6. And it was an important factor in Bletchley's success in breaking German ciphers promptly and regularly. It was particularly important in the case of Enigma machine cipher, the main cipher used for secret communication in the higher army and air force echelons down to regiment and *staffel* and from naval vessels.

The Enigma cipher machine looked at first sight rather like a typewriter. It had a keyboard of 26 letters but no stops, numerals or operating procedures. When a letter was struck, a letter different from the struck letter showed in an illuminated panel. If you continued to type out the clear text and write down what showed in the panel, you got your cipher text. Put the machine back to the original position at the start of the message and type out your cipher text - and you had your clear text. This admirably simple system to operate, had two essential features, which were in fact weaknesses from a security point of view. These were reciprocity - the fact that coding and decoding were achieved by the same process - and exclusivity, the fact that no letter could stay the same when encoded.

In its simplest form an Enigma machine comprised the keyboard and the panel of lights and in between them a scrambler consisting of an entry wheel with 26 terminals, three rotors each with 26 contacts wired to a different point on its other side and a reflector wheel with 26 contacts cross-connected in pairs. Striking a key moved one rotor on and sent a current through the rotors to the reflector and back through the rotors to the illuminated panel. The other rotors moved on as in a cyclometer once in every revolution of the previous rotor - making $26^3$ different encoding positions in all for each rotor combination. Each rotor was encircled by an adjustable ring which could be locked on to it in any one of 26 positions indicated by letters on its rim. Key instructions for the day consisted of rotor order (a choice of six with three rotors) and ring settings - indicated by three letters. There were thus, 6 x $26^3$ possible settings or just over a hundred thousand, not an impossible task even by trial and error, if the wiring of the wheels was known. However quite early in the thirties a major complication was introduced. Ten pairs of letters were cross-plugged so that the entry and exit points of each pair of letters to and from the scrambler were interchanged. There are some 40 million million ways of doing this. Then in 1938 the numbers of different rotors issued with each machine was increased from three to five, thus increasing possible rotor orders from 6 to 60.

So by the beginning of the war each machine was issued with the same standard five rotors and had a choice of 60 different permutations for the three which it used. To read an Enigma message what was needed was the setting for the day, which changed at midnight and consisted of *walzen* (choice of rotors), *ringstellung* (position of rings) and *stecker* (cross plugging); and the setting for the individual message or part message, consisting of an indicator of three letters, telling where to position the wheels at the start of the message. And of course the indicator was itself enciphered.

It was a two stage operation. The sender picked three letters for his open indicator and three for his secret indicator. Next he put his three rotors in the open indicator position and enciphered the secret indicator and in his preamble to the message put the open indicator followed by encipherment of the secret indicator. Then he set his rotors according to the secret indicator and tapped out the enciphered message. The cipher being reciprocal, the recipient just set his rotors by the open indicator, deciphered the secret indicator, set his rotors accordingly, tapped away and out came the clear message. All this was simple enough if you had the day's setting. Without knowing it however, you had to try 60 different rotor orders, $26^3$ different ring settings and about 40 million million possible cross plugging arrangements.

Yet by the mid thirties the Poles had developed the basic principles of unravelling this maze and had actually made some breaks while the number of rotors was still only three and thus the possible different rotor orders only six. How they got hold of an Enigma machine is disputed but it is difficult to believe that they reconstructed one cryptoanalytically from a study of the traffic. But once they had the machine they found two basic approaches each of which enabled them to bypass tackling the 40 million million possible cross pluggings and concentrate on reducing the hundred thousand or so possible combinations of rotor order and ring settings to a manageable number of likelies The two approaches were by 'sillies' and by 'cribs'. Both relied on the exploitation of German tidy - mindedness and love of neat short-cuts. 'Sillies' were give-aways of the ring settings and/or secret indicators. For example similarity in the open indicators of first messages of the day from different stations could suggest that they had not moved their rotors much since setting the rings. Again keyboard patterns in the open indicators of multi-part messages might suggest interpolations for the secret indicators, thus providing leads which were both sillies (giving away part of the setting) and cribs (informed guesses of the clear text corresponding to part of the cipher text, in this case the enciphered indicator).

This second method through cribs was in the upshot to prove much the most important.

Fortunately a flying start to Polish 'cribbing' was provided by the German decision to encipher their secret indicators twice, presumably in order to ensure that the recipient got it right. These repeats were in fact very strong cribs. That the actual letters of the secret indicator were not revealed did not matter. The cross-plugging would in any case obscure the absolute points of entry of current to the rotors. But relativities were a different matter. The fact that there were three repeats of letters each three taps on was unaffected by cross-plugging and provided information compatible with only a few wheel orders and ring settings.

Tests of such compatibility could be devised. The most obvious was to plan and carry out a sort of daisy chain of successive encipherments which were based on the phasing (number of tap spaces) between repeats and should lead back to the original letter. This involved testing in this way all possible rotor orders and ring settings and was much too slow by hand, though it looked possible to design a machine to do it at speed for cribs of all kinds. So for the particular leads provided by the repeated indicators, they found a method which after massive preparatory work gave quick results by hand. They prepared perforated sheets showing the distribution for each rotor order of places in which some letters of the enciphered indicator, as well as the secret indicator repeated and they compared these with the actual distribution of such repeats in the intercepted enciphered indicators.

When in the late thirties the Germans increased the number of rotors from three to five and so the number of rotor orders from 6 to 60, Polish resources proved inadequate to the increased demands for preparatory work. However in August 1939 they managed just in time to hand over to the British an Enigma machine with 5 rotors, some old decodes, the perforated sheets with which they had obtained their earlier success and preliminary designs for an electrical testing machine or 'bombe' for breaking Enigma on 'cribs', i.e. informed guesses of the clear text of some messages.

This precious gift was collected by a secret department of the Foreign Office, the Government Code and Cipher School which under its cover name Government Communications was in process of putting itself on an expanded war time footing both by recruitment, largely of post-graduates from Cambridge and Oxford, and by acquiring a suitable large country house and grounds - Bletchley Park in Buckinghamshire.

Among the recruits to Bletchley Park in 1939 was Gordon Welchman, a mathematics don from Sidney Sussex Cambridge. He was given the task of analysing the German call sign system, and told nothing about the Poles' cryptographic work. However he worked out for himself how after adequate preparation Enigma might be broken currently on the double indicators and took his solution to Dilly Knox, the doyen of the old cryptographic establishment. Dilly was apparently a little miffed that Gordon had found out all this by himself and told him that everything was in hand and to go back to his call sign analysis. Work on call signs brought Gordon into contact with the intercept stations so that he got an overall impression of the scale and pattern of the radio communications of the German armed forces. He now realised that the cryptographic establishment were still thinking too small and too slow and he formed a comprehensive plan to achieve and exploit fully the current breaking of Enigma. In the spring of 1940 he put his proposals to Travis, the Director of Bletchley Park, who accepted them. A cryptographic watch working round the clock was established in Hut 6 and an intelligence watch in Hut 3 to translate and annotate the decodes and forward their contents with the source suitably disguised. The plan also provided for staff for sorting the incoming traffic and staff and machines for decoding messages as well as for research cryptographers working on as yet unbroken keys and for designers and engineers working on the development of machinery to help breaking, e.g. the 'bombe' for high speed testing of wheel order and ring settings for compatibility with information from cribs. Looking further ahead the plan also covered the staffing maintenance and operation of the bombes, when developed and installed. The intercept stations, both air force and military were expanded to meet Bletchley's needs and continuously advised by Hut 6 after consultation with Hut 3 of Bletchley's requirements. Despatch of messages from intercept stations was speeded up, at first by despatch rider and then increasingly by teleprinter.

By the summer of 1940 much of the reorganisation on these lines had taken place. The perforated sheets for the breaking of Enigma from indicator repeats had been completed and current breaking of the main German air force key had started. The whole complex system was moving into gear and intelligence poured out.

Then suddenly came disaster. The Germans dropped repeating their indicators on the invasion of France. The breaks already made had shown it was not difficult to find cribs, i.e. to pick out messages whose addresses, signatures and main headings were likely to be written according to a predictable formula which varied little from day to day. Among the most famous of these messages was *Befehl fuer die kampffuerung* (Orders for bomber command), but air force traffic was thick with long forms of address and signature and situation, weather and other regular reports which, if times and days of sending were added according to formulae, provided quite long cribs. Moreover the Germans would actually send tuning messages, identifiable as such by the interceptor from the procedure, and include in the message the phrase *Dieses ist ein abstimnspruch* (This is a tuning message) enciphered in Enigma. But working on cribs by hand was so slow as to be impractical and none of the 'bombes' to do the job at speed were yet operational. Fortunately German tidy mindedness and Hut 6 inspiration came to the rescue. Day after day the Germans provided sillies. Day after day Hut 6 found them and got out 'Red', the German Air Force key. By these daily miracles the breaks continued until the first 'bombe' was ready. The bombe was a device for testing rapidly all combinations and positions of the rotors to find those consistent with information from the crib. Once the rotor combination and position were found, ring setting and cross-plugging could be deduced. The bombe consisted of a series of simple Enigma machines (without cross plugging) all loaded with the same rotors in the same order which were rotated together at the same high speed and electrically programmed to stop on attempting an electric circuit consistent with certain relative positions of the contacts connecting the machines. These relative positions were based on a menu or programme consisting of a chain of connections formed by using letters that occurred more than once in either cipher text or crib, as the spaces between these were unaffected by the *stecker* (cross-plugging). The reciprocal nature of Enigma made it possible to use links in either direction, cipher text to crib or crib to cipher text, to form a sort of daisy chain which looped back to its starting point. The longer and more complex the chain the stronger and more economical in bombe time was the menu, but the greater the risk of failure through interception error or crib mis-phrasing.

In some comparatively rare cases, where Enigma machines were used without a *stecker* or only a few letters were swapped or the *stecker* was known (e.g. with the 'Orange; see p.52) it was possible to break on quite a short crib - five or even sometimes three letters - without the bombe by working through the wheels one at a time with tables based on the connections in the wheel and watching for evidence of a consistent result. With a five letter crib the chances of getting positive evidence were about the same as for getting a pair or better in a first deal at poker.

The position then was simple. Enigma could be rapidly broken with a crib. It was therefore essential to find cribs, to identify the 'stars' on which they were passed, to get those stars properly covered at the intercept stations (there could be as much as a seven-fold cover on a crib message) and rapidly sent to Bletchley, to position the crib correctly in relation to the cipher text and to write menus for the bombe. By the summer of 1940 Hut 6 at Bletchley was already starting to do all these things effectively. Messages sent to Bletchley from the intercept stations were sorted first by type of cipher. The army and air force Enigma messages went to Hut 6, where they were sorted into piles according to the 'discriminants' (see p.36) indicating their cipher setting: and their preambles and the call signs and frequencies of the stations passing them were recorded on lists called 'blists' for each setting concerned. Preambles consisted of time of origin, urgency prefix (kr) if any, indicator (letters giving the starting position of the encodement) and the number of letters in the message and the first five letter group, including the discriminant. Fortunately the Germans greatly assisted the identification of discriminants for each key and hence the sorting of messages into keys by using two or more discriminants on multi-part messages.

The Hut 6 watch would go into the big blist room to pick out the crib messages. Many of these stood out well on the blist by reason of the frequencies on which they were passed, their times of origin and sending, and the number of stations receiving them. The crib messages were then got out of their respective piles and handed round the watch to be worked on. Here the exclusivity of Enigma, the fact that no letter could go to itself, i.e. stay unchanged in the cipher test, came in useful. It limited the number of positions in which a crib could be fitted to the cipher text to those without a 'crash', i.e. a letter going to itself. And these were quite few in a crib of twenty five letters, while, if a crib of forty letters could be fitted without a crash, there was a strong presumption that it was the right clear text and correctly positioned.

Having tested various versions of the crib in various positions, the cryptographer would pick one or two likely ones and write his menus. These were fed into the bombe and with any luck anything from a few minutes to a few hours later the bombe would stop at a position, which when examined was right. The settings and the whole pile of messages to be decoded would then be passed to the decoding room. The decoded messages would be sent through at once to the Hut 3 watch, which would amend them (there were often gaps and errors owing to poor reception) and would make annotated translations and comments which would be forwarded to the few destinations entitled to receive Ultra.

So much for the main stream of Enigma army and air force messages, which, when I was at Bletchley, were flowing along on conveyor belts. But there were also eddies from the main stream. First of all, the settings which were unbroken went to cryptographic research parties. Secondly, the duds, i.e. the messages which were sorted into the pile for a setting that was broken but failed to come out in the decoding room, went to research parties who tried again to decode them or to find out why they could not be decoded. They would check if the message had been rightly classified and sorted and they would look for variant forms of the 'indicator', the three letters which showed the starting position of the rotors.

Besides this whole complex dealing with Enigma messages sent by the German army and air force, there were other cryptographic sections at Bletchley. Enigma message sent by the German navy were dealt with in Hut 8 and Hut 4 whose successes became a vital factor in hunting down submarines. Then there was the party dealing with *Geheimschreiber* (or 'Fish' as we called it) a sort of high speed scrambled radio teleprinting, used for a few urgent high level messages. I had little to do with either the naval or 'Fish' parties. Finally there were the sections dealing with hand ciphers and codes. Some of these were sent on the same 'stars' as army and air force Enigma and accordingly I had occasion to have dealings with them and know a little of their problems. They also liked to find cribs.

# HELPING THE CRYPTOGRAPHERS

The cryptographic organisation at Bletchley was highly efficient. Indeed it was the most efficient working organisation I have met, perhaps because there were no trade unions and little or no financial control and because it was run mainly neither by business men nor career civil servants but by mathematicians and chess players, who brought detached and decisive minds to the solution of cryptographic organisational and human problems. Contributory factors were the devotion, high morale and esprit de corps of the picked band of workers. Gifted people were willing to work on boring and repetitive tasks if it was important that these should be done by people capable of spotting the occasional small nugget, which might turn up in the sieve. For after all we were prospecting for something more precious than gold. An interesting symptom of Bletchley's efficiency was the small size of the central administrative staff which was the servant of the operational chiefs and not their master, as is too often the case in peace-time civil service departments.

Nevertheless in spite of Bletchley's efficiency, it was clear to me, as it had been to Welchman and Milner-Barry that our party had much to offer the cryptographers. Our communications picture, based on both logs and decodes and thus on an outline of the total working of each 'star' was different from, and complementary to, theirs which was based on the sorting of messages into keys and settings. We therefore formed a natural link between cryptographers and could offer them specific services. On Hut 6 blists, the big operational messages relayed on several stars showed up clearly and those of them that served as cribs were often unmistakable. But there were other routine messages, which were not so easy to spot on the blists, but were obvious in the folders of log readers' summaries, where one could follow the star's operational procedures repeating day after day. We were thus able to help Hut 6 to spot certain cribs and to call the attention of Hut 6 researchers to routine messages in an unbroken key, which might well prove to be useful cribs, once one day's settings were broken.

Another service which we could give was to help in getting out the 'duds', the messages which did not make sense when decoded on the settings to which they had been classified. The chat about message checking on the logs could help in some of these cases either to get the message out or to suggest that it was in a different setting or to show that the German recipients themselves could not make head or tail of it. At the same time the Hut 6 section dealing with duds and cipher texts generally were in a position to contribute to radio intelligence by tracing retransmissions of messages on different networks.

Then again chat or messages in code or hand cipher on the logs might compromise part of an Enigma setting. This was rare but could be very important as in the case of the experimental signals regiment (see pp.35-36) or in the extraordinary case of the SS 'star' to concentration camps. In addition to Enigma messages in their own key, which we called 'Orange', these camps each sent a daily return - number of interns at the beginning of the day, number received, number dead or transferred, number at end of day - a chilling little tally. These returns were sent not in clear but in a simple substitution code with a letter for each digit. This code was changed daily but with the first number of the following day always the same as the last number of the previous day it broke itself. To his amazement the Hut 6 cryptographer found that if the day's substitution code was written out against the ten digits in order, the five pairs of letters were the *stecker* instructions for the current day's Enigma; Orange had only five pairs of letters swapped instead of the usual ten pairs. This prime example of Germans using a pattern to hand meant that Orange could be broken without recourse to the bombe and on a short crib (see p.48).

However much the most important service, which we could give the cryptographers was to suggest re-encodements and this service became increasingly important.

Re-encodements of a message from a key already broken are clearly likely to provide an excellent crib and were used by Hut 6 from the first. There were for example re-encodements from one day's setting into the next day's setting. Obviously once everyone had changed the settings on their machines, it was easier for the Germans to repeat the message in the new setting to anyone who had somehow missed it. Indeed the fact that this was a re-encodement of a message first sent on the previous day was sometimes underlined by giving two times of origin in the preamble - one being the original time of origin and the second the time of the re-encodement.

Then there were re-encodements from one Enigma key into another and from Enigma to a hand cipher. Our log readers with their summaries of all communications on each star were in much the best position to spot such re-encodements. Hut 6 had in fact managed to pick out some re-encodements just by pairing messages with the same time or origin and approximately the same number of letters. But this was very hit and miss and tended to waste bombe time. We were in a position to suggest Enigma to Enigma re-encodements with much greater confidence, while the relatively rare instances of re-encodements between Enigma and a hand cipher could normally only be spotted from the logs.

Accordingly, as soon as I came to Bletchley, I began to visit Hut 6 research sections with suggestions about routine messages chat and other traffic on the logs, duds and re-encodements. And gradually I got into the habit of visiting Hut 6 watch and the blist room as well. As the need for them grew and was appreciated, regular services to Hut 6 were built up. These services became more and more important as Hut 6, by then headed by Stuart Milner-Barry, started to face new problems.

These problems were of two kinds - difficulties of sorting and identification and cryptographic complications. The number of different settings used daily increased, particularly after the Normandy landings; and it became more difficult to find routine messages which provided regular cribs in all of them. The way in had to come more often from a re-encodement. Fortunately as the number of keys increased, so did the number of re-encodements which we could spot on the logs. There were quite a lot of cases, where one station on a star had not got the same key as the others and day after day messages would be re-encoded to it.

With this sort of help, Hut 6 continued to break the bulk of air force and army Enigma messages pretty promptly in spite of new difficulties. Late in 1944 the German army and air force stopped using discriminants (see p. 36) and it was no longer possible for Hut 6 to tell just by looking at the first group of a message what its setting was and into which pile it should be sorted. They had to sort on the call-sign book column of the call sign of the sender or recipient, identify the 'stars' from their call sign column and frequency and on this basis hunt for crib messages and re-encodements. Later sorting became still more difficult because the air force stopped using call signs from the predictable call-sign book columns (see pp. 31-32) I made a catalogue of known 'stars' their frequencies and characteristics, which was helpful to the log reader and perhaps to the intercept stations and Hut 6 research but it was little use to Hut 6 watch, who only had the Enigma messages and could not wait till we received the logs. They continued to sort by call sign column and to link certain columns together from their use on the same star or on stars linked by message retransmissions. In this way they kept up right until VE Day a volume of messages decoded within a few hours or at worst a day of their transmission, though the number of duds to be dealt with increased. In fact from the Battle of Britain to VE day, Hut 6 never failed for a single day to break Red, usually by 8 o'clock in the morning - and in spite of the proliferation of keys, Red, the Luftwaffe *masehinenschuluessel*, continued to be widely used and remained the most important source not only about the GAF but generally.

Hut 6 achieved this in spite not only of these problems of sorting but also of complications of the Enigma cipher itself. During the last year of the war, the German armed forces first put a new *unkerwaltz* (reflector wheel) into the Enigma machine and then later started to change the *unkerwaltze* connections daily as part of the daily cipher setting. The first problem was tackled by Dr Aitken, the Scottish chess champion, who worked on it for three days, while to deal with the second the Bletchley mathematicians, amongst others Welchman and Turing and Alexander (from the naval section) got together and designed an electronic computer.

The hand cipher cryptographers also had some new problems in the last years of the war. The Germans started to use 'Stencil', the kind of cipher in which you write your message along the rows of a pad that looks like a crossword puzzle form and then take out the columns in a pre-arranged order. This is a very difficult cipher to break even with a crib if the pattern of the crossword form is wholly unpredictable. Fortunately the Germans simplified the task with their passion for system and economy of means. They decided to construct their stencil forms out of just 28 different lines. All stencil pads were just arrangements of a selection of these lines. The difficulty presented by Stencil was thus greatly reduced.

I was from time to time able to help the hand cipher cryptographers by suggesting a re-encodement from a broken cipher (usually Enigma), by calling attention to traffic on the same star in a broken cipher or simply by identifying some of the units involved so that signatures and addresses could be guessed.

## CONTRIBUTIONS TO INTELLIGENCE

I was the Central Party's link with the cryptographers. Our direct contribution to intelligence and our service to the Hut 3 watch were not my business, but that of my brother officers, notably Edward Rushworth, the Yorkshireman with the encyclopaedic memory, who sat beside me at a big shared desk and helped to keep it clear - I have always been hopeless at controlling papers.

So on this side of the work I do not know much detail. Painting with a broad brush, I would like to emphasise first that it is impossible to evaluate separately the contributions of cryptography and radio intelligence. They were so interdependent. Working with addresses, signatures and radio operating instructions from the decodes and with diagrams of stars' working summarised from the logs, the Central Party at Bletchley with the aid of some rather imprecise direction finding built up pictures of different parts of the radio network of the German army and air force - the frequencies and call signs used and the identities and locations of the Units using them. One officer in the fusion room was occupied in putting all this information together on a huge map, which was described by a visiting general as the most complete German order of battle he had seen anywhere. It was in fact only a skeleton, if a complete one. The flesh and blood of strengths in men and materials, the sinews of war, we left to the Hut 3 indexers. Nevertheless the shape of this skeleton and in particular changes in its shape yielded important information both directly and by providing the

Hut 3 watch with material for notes on the decodes. Direct intelligence from the Central Party was mainly of the broad strategic kind. The establishment of new networks even if they did not pass much traffic and the movement of stations to new areas heralded the development of new strategies, new major campaigns. The imminence of the German attacks on Russia and the Balkans, and of the German campaign in North Africa were all indicated in this way.

On the other hand, radio intelligence units in the field, particularly in North Africa, provided much prompt tactical intelligence. They were close enough to the enemy transmitters to receive signals direct rather than bounced off the Heavyside layer. So they got undistorted bearings and precise fixes and could follow the movement of stations accurately and currently. The Ultra signals based on Enigma decodes, inevitably came in much later, even when the keys were in Cairo (see p.37). And even when they came, they might not contain the vital information on location and movement.

Nevertheless this very useful radio intelligence owed much of its precision to earlier Enigma breaks which identified the units associated with each transmitter. What the radio intelligence unit did was to recognise the stations in spite of daily change of call signs and follow their movements. Sometimes too the actual intercept operator made a valuable contribution. For example in the winter of 1940/41, while we were still half expecting an invasion of Britain, an intercept operator picked up a signal from a new station with an operator, whom he recognised from his touch as one who had been active on a network in France. Cross bearings on the new station yielded a location on the Baltic coast, while the old network was found to be still active in France but sending what were obviously spoof messages in the practice key, which we called Blue. So we concluded that the Germans were giving up the invasion and starting to move units east, while trying to hide the move. This was perhaps the first strong indication from any source that the invasion was off.

An important part of the Central Party's work was our service to Hut 3. Usually in answer to enquiries, we would identify senders and recipients of messages, where these were not given in the decode or were not all or not clearly given (perhaps because the intercepted message had been too faint or muffled to take down accurately). And we might give other background information such as location and place in the network. To provide a fast radio intelligence advice service, Rodney Bax and later Basil Malabre were moved into Hut 3. While the call sign systems which we had broken and captured were being used, the call sign on the message pad might be enough to provide the required information; but if there was time, it was always better to consult the logs.

I think I should conclude this section by quoting the one clear example I remember when the Central Party and Hut 3 failed to pass on vital information. It is such a text book illustration both of the sort of thing which radio intelligence can contribute and of how vital intelligence can fail to get through if people are afraid to speak up because it is not their place. Such timidity was very unlike the usual attitudes in Bletchley. It is, as I have said, the only such occasion I can remember.

It was December 1944 and the German armies appeared to be in full retreat, when Rushworth and I read a message setting up a new 'star' on which were all the armoured divisions, including some transferred from the Russian front. They were given orders to maintain wireless silence apart from occasional calling and keying to keep in touch, keying that should never go on long enough for a bearing on the station to be taken. They did just that. The intercept stations were told to listen on the announced frequency and they picked up the announced call signs and a little keying at intervals but nothing else. At a meeting of officers of our unit, we considered whether to tell Hut 3 that this looked rather like preparation for a counter offensive. I was all for telling but the meeting decided not to for the rather poor reason that it would make a big fuss and we would look so silly if we were wrong. A few days later came the Ardennes offensive for which the Allies were unprepared.

I talked about this later with Peter Calvocoressi, the head of Air Intelligence section in Hut 3, and he told me not to feel too badly about it, as Hut 3 already suspected from increases in railway traffic and other indications. Then why did not Supreme Headquarters Allied Expeditionary Force know? I asked, Peter explained that Hut 3 was shy of going beyond its job of amending and explaining German messages. Drawing broad conclusions was for the intelligence staff at SHAEF, who had information from all sources. So Hut 3 did not tell SHAEF of the conclusions they were beginning to draw and SHAEF did not draw any conclusions, as is clear from Winterbotham's book *The Ultra Secret*, where he states there was no evidence of the enemy offensive from Bletchley or anywhere else.

Peter Calvocoressi, in his book *Top Secret Ultra*, gives a different account, quoting the story of the announcement of the new network as an example of valuable radio intelligence, as if I had actually told him in time. I'm sure I should have, even though it was not my job. I knew him and I should have told him the facts and asked his opinion. But at the time I didn't. Nor, I think, can Bax or Malabre have commented on the message announcement as this would have been enough to put Winterbotham's staff on their guard. I still feel badly about it. It was so unlike Bletchley. And it cost lives.

# CO-OPERATION WITH THE RUSSIANS

There were no Russians at Bletchley and it was quite out of the question to tell the Russians anything which would lead them to suspect Bletchley's cryptographic success. Their security was too poor and they could have compromised the whole operation. Their ciphers were broken regularly by the Germans as we knew from decoded messages of the German *Abwehr*. We warned them of the vulnerability of their ciphers, concealing the source of our information and letting them get hot under the collar, believing that we, their ally, were monitoring and breaking their traffic.

Similarly the key points in the massive volume of intelligence from Enigma about German dispositions and plans on the Eastern Front had to be fed to them with the source well disguised.

Accordingly Edward Crankshaw, sent to represent signals intelligence with the British military mission to Moscow was not in a good position to arrange a large- scale exchange of intelligence. He tried feeding them with a few little bits of information in the hope that they would reciprocate - which they never did. However in the end they did come up with the present of a second copy of the German Air Force call sign book, which we had already both reconstructed and captured.

# THE END OF THE AFFAIR

After the German surrender, Bletchley Park put on a terrific VE party, a fancy dress ball with oceans to drink, a top band, our own cabaret, special decor, soft lights, and all the trimmings. It must have been quite one of the best end-of-war parties, almost as good as VJ day in the Friendly Islands.

And then most of us began to unwind and relax, think what to do next and find something to do, while we were thinking. A number of us, myself included, were put on to the quiet task of writing a history of some aspect of Bletchley's work in the war. I cannot remember in detail what I wrote then - it has got somewhat blurred after forty years. But I know that I stressed then, as I have now, that radio intelligence and cryptography must work closely together - so closely that they are practically one. I felt it important to stress this point because I had recently been visited by an army officer from the section of counter-intelligence responsible for radio security. He put such security in a totally different category from cipher security, which he was not prepared to discuss. In vain I said 'The attack has to be integrated. And so surely must defence be.' He could not, he said, include such a point in his report.

What I did not stress then, because I did not realise it fully, was how unusual and unusually efficient a working organisation Bletchley Park in fact was. I have since found that my rigid military visitor was just a foretaste of the stupidities I would meet in the world outside.

I decided to leave the Park by the end of the year like many of my friends, a number of whom have since had brilliant careers. I worked for a magazine chain and investigated for them the pretentious and arrogant world of design consultants. I was taken on as a report writer by management consultants and got an insight into the incredibly uniform pattern of inefficiency in post-war British industry. From 1947 to 1976, however, I worked quietly in a backwater of the Central Office of Information, trying to present to the world abroad a balanced and truthful picture of the British economy, institutions and way of life which would highlight the good points but could never be proved to omit important black spots. I wrestled with extracting information from different government departments and reconciling their conflicting comments and statistics, sat through long and intensely boring trade union and joint committees, and sympathised increasingly with departmental establishment divisions, sandwiched between the trade unions and the Treasury and the Civil Service Department, tied to the rigid interpretation of an over-elaborate rule book and therefore almost bound to empire-build and expand in order to cope and defend themselves. I now look back on Bletchley Park not, I hope, with rose-coloured spectacles, but with a vision sharpened by the contrast with everything I have known since.

# Part II

# About Neil Webster

Neil Webster was a very intelligent man, a brilliant mathematician, a classical scholar, a linguist, literate and artistic, widely read and politically aware, liberal, agnostic, courteous, civilized, charming and very kind. His family, friends and colleagues remember him in later life as a sort of Bertrand Russell character – with a mane of silver hair, penetrating blue eyes, a quizzical look, and an immediate enthusiasm for any discussion or argument or challenge. (Apparently the Webster children inherited his love of argument: get the family together in a room and they immediately dive into heated discussion while ignoring practical matters, to the despair of everyone else around!) Neil had a sharp wit, a delight in the absurdities of life – and a habit of quoting from classics or French literature during conversation, with an expectant air of sharing a known punch line, as if everyone knew what he meant (which one seldom did). He had no "side" and was never embarrassed or class conscious, was vague and untidy, and quite impractical.

But at the time that the events in *Cribs for Victory* occurred, Neil was a man in his early thirties with a strong original mind, and a restless maverick spirit, unsettled in life.

Neil Leslie Webster was born on November 7th 1906 in his grandparents' home, in Merionethshire, Wales. The Websters were a Scottish family, many of whom had served in the Indian Civil Service. Flora Annie Webster had married a cousin, Hal Steel and gone with him straight to India, almost as a child bride. Over the years she had taken up women's rights there, started writing about India, and become justly famous – for her writings and her outspoken views. " Can't you control that wife of yours, Steel?" his superior officer once asked  –  and received the famous reply, "Take her for a week, old boy, and try!".

Flora and Hal, when retired, had taken a 14-year lease on a house called 'Talgarth' near Machynlleth, surrounded by beautiful bluebell woods. Their daughter Mabel had married her first cousin, Jack Webster, who also joined the Indian Civil Service, and the pair had immediately left for India. Three years later Mabel returned to England to give birth to a son - Neil's brother Patrick, born in 1903. Three and a half years later she returned again and according to Flora Annie's account in her autobiography *The Garden of Fidelity* "another son put in an appearance: it was also born at home, under our roof... Since then both children have entered largely into my life, for we have had charge of them during their parents' absence in India. They have been an immense pleasure."

Flora Annie was a powerful influence on Neil's life. As a celebrated author and campaigner, she moved in influential literary circles in Britain, was a friend of Ruskin, and knew established political and artistic figures (her sister-in-law had married Augustus John). The household was accustomed to discussion and campaigning and philosophical debate, and the young Neil was exposed to this. Like any child of absent parents, he spent vacations and occasional longer periods staying with various family connections - whether his father's sister, the artist Adelaide 'Lally' Donald (née Webster) and her four stepsons or Augustus John's extraordinarily intense and radical family - and developed independence of mind very early.

Flora Annie describes an incident from his childhood in wartime. "My daughter, prevented from joining her husband in India, went nursing... I fed the schoolchildren and amused them by burning an effigy of the German Emperor on Guy Fawkes Day... Later, I am in a railway carriage. I am telling a story of my youngest grandchild to a woman, fat, fair and forty, dressed in a plenitude of black bugles. 'The child,' I said, 'he is but seven, was playing but his face was all serious'. 'Neil,' I said, 'what are you thinking of?' He looked up: 'They say your heart is where your treasure is – well! I wish I were where I want to be.' 'And where's that?' I asked, thinking that perhaps the child's mind was with his parents. He looked at me coolly and replied 'Beside the German Emperor with my pistol at his head'. So he went on playing."

Flora also describes how, in support of the suffragette movement, she withheld her rates on the cottage they owned by the sea and how her goods were then auctioned and her publisher bid a lot of money for the first chapter of her novel *On the Face of the Waters* and the villagers all came to the auction; presumably Neil came too. When women finally got the vote she and Mabel (then in India) sent each other cables, each saying "Victory!"

As a boy, having been found to have a heart 'murmur', Neil's education was largely by governesses – who, as he later ruefully admitted, he drove to distraction and near nervous breakdowns by his constant questions and argumentativeness. Private tutoring followed for three to four years; this in itself explains the unusual quality of Neil's thinking

In 1920 Flora moved to Cheltenham, "where my youngest grandson had won a scholarship." At Cheltenham College from autumn 1920 to April 1925 he was in the Classical Department: the syllabus covered English, Latin, Greek, French, Mathematics, History, Geography, German, and the sciences. Flora relates how Neil produced a Greek play, and she came to help with the scenery! At Cheltenham he was discovered to be exceptionally quick at maths, having a natural aptitude for numbers, logic and abstract reasoning.

In 1925 Neil, having won a place at Corpus Christi College, Oxford, left Cheltenham and took a year out, when he seems to have continued to study maths and logic and visited his brother Patrick in Paris, becoming virtually bilingual in French. In 1926 Neil's parents Jack and Mabel Webster retired and settled in Cheltenham. Neil took up the place at Oxford in autumn 1926, to study Logic with Greats. Flora Annie then went to Jamaica, accompanied by Neil who was then 21 and still at Oxford. "She told me," said Neil, "she had packed her shroud". The Webster family had an estate at Cousins Cove, Jamaica. Flora Annie had been there some years earlier to sort out a legal challenge to ownership. However this time Neil and Flora were much feted out there. "We stayed with the Deputy Governor who gave an enormous party for us and we toured the beautiful island in a Model T Ford with a black chauffeur called Nethersole."

Back in England, Flora Annie, though now in her late seventies, spent time in Neil's college at Oxford researching a book in the Bodleian. Neil finished his degree, graduating as BA Hons. Literare Humaniores, in 1929. In that same year, Flora Annie died.

Neil then decided to move on to Cambridge, to the (identically named) Corpus Christi College there, to study something more practical - doing a post-graduate course in Industrial Psychology - and hoping to get a job in industrial management. However he soon found that in tough economic conditions no one in British management was interested in such niceties while fending off bankruptcy, and after one assignment he became disillusioned with the whole idea. Perhaps motivated by his earlier happy experiences there, he set out for America. His friend James Donald, who subsequently became a film star, best known for his role as Major Clipton, the doctor in the film *The Bridge On The River Kwai*, recalls:

"My favourite picture is of his arrival at our front door in Montreal [Canada] in a roofless drop-head coupe without windows or windscreen driven by an ebullient chap called Postlethwaite who made a bee-line for my stepmother and almost charmed the knickers off her, not an easy thing to do. This was at the time when Neil was selling beer-filters all over America. (In six months he did sell one!). I went with them across town to a garage and learned that they had driven out from New York and overturned on the ice at about halfway on the trip in a temperature around 0°F, whereupon they turned the car right side up and drove on. The journey to the garage was the coldest cold I ever experienced. Postlethwaite was not a slow driver."

After travelling around and trying various jobs, and spending some time involved in the literary scene in New York, Neil established a bar/restaurant at Daytona Beach in Florida with a partner who was a chef. Apparently, according to one of his colleagues in the COI, Neil said that when the Bluebird tried for the land speed record on Daytona Beach in March 1935 he, having a student pilot's licence, organized flights over the beach for customers at the bar to see the sight! Because of the recession the bar was not a financial success and after three years collapsed when the partner disappeared with all the remaining money.

As he says in *Cribs for Victory* he then returned to England and worked rather unsuccessfully as a literary agent, although he did once say that he turned down an offer from Allen Lane to go into partnership producing cheap paperbacks "because he was advised it was a poor risk!"

Neil had been told by his literary agent friends in Cheltenham that there was a young woman, Elizabeth (Betty) Heygate, he should meet who was trying to be a musician and writer and possibly had talent.

Elizabeth relates her first impressions: "I was confronted one morning when I opened the door to an imperious ring, by a small man in a black overcoat down to his ankles and a black homburg hat, in which he looked like a cross between Jimmy Cagney and Humphrey Bogart. (His stay in America had made him affect Chicago gangster style).

'Er-' he said.

'Not today, thank you!' I retorted and slammed the door in his face."

That might have been the end of that, but Neil was nothing if not persistent. When next he appeared, still in his long black coat, she was trying to avoid a lovesick suitor, and he offered her his arm.

Elizabeth continues: "It was the start of something I couldn't make head or tail of ... and couldn't handle either... I was totally bewildered by this extraordinary man. To begin with, he was thirty and I was seventeen. He was (in my eyes) clever, sophisticated, disillusioned and anti-romantic (so I thought!). He had a cool, logical brain and an intensely argumentative nature – and he couldn't abide shams or sentimental clichés. He was, he admitted the kind of little boy who pulled the wings off flies to see what they were made of – and he was still pulling them off metaphorically speaking – and he has been ever since!"

Neil, for his part, admitted that as soon as he met her, he was "a goner!" bowled over "hook line and sinker!"

Elizabeth (Betty) Marjorie Heygate was born July 13th 1918, daughter of Marjorie Rennie, a Newfoundland belle and Lancelot Heygate, a civil engineer who worked all over the world, son of Reverend Ambrose Heygate and Jeannie McNab. Elizabeth was brought up by her grandparents in Congleton rectory, as her parents were abroad, and then divorced, in her childhood. She shared Neil's independence of mind, a result of early separation from parents, but was otherwise a total contrast to him – romantic, passionate, brought up with church values of conventional morality, creative, dramatic, an aspiring writer, loving the theatre, and studying music in Cheltenham.

Elizabeth continues "He was used to intellectual argument, from his earliest years when he walked with Henry John and discussed the Theory of Relativity, - to Oxford and then Cambridge. And then there were his family. All of them were used to pure intellectual argument just for the fun of it – particularly Neil's mother, Mabel. The Websters had a pleasant house in Cheltenham in Albert Road, with the gardens running down to a gate into Pittville Park near the lake. On my first visit, they forgot me and had a colossal argument about the Milk Marketing Board... and I sat, feeling very small, while conversational ping-pong shot round me from all sides.."

In late 1936, Neil ended up in the Radcliffe Infirmary at Oxford with a broken pelvis after a car crash (he always had to wear adapted handmade shoes after this, but it never stopped him nimbly dancing the Charleston at parties or the Scottish sword dance on New Year's Eve!). He returned to London in early 1937, on crutches and two of Neil's friends – James Donald and Tony Pirie - then persuaded Elizabeth to move there too. She took a job, studied music and lived in a flat in Pimlico near Neil's rooms in Warwick Square. When Elizabeth's father, Lancelot, died young, his health broken by drink and the failure of his marriage, Neil stood by her and dealt with all the practicalities. Back in London their life was "swinging with gaiety, modern, intellectual, and racy – as the shadow of the Nazi regime grew".

In autumn 1938, Neil and Elizabeth got engaged. In spring 1939 he decided to join the London Scottish Reserve. " This surprised me rather" Elizabeth comments " - he was not at all a warlike man". Fearing that he would be posted abroad, Neil and Elizabeth married on September 13th 1939 – just a few days after the outbreak of war.

As he relates, it was the loyalty of his friends in the London Scottish, particularly Nigel Burgess, that got him into Intelligence, after he handled a routine desk task badly. When he was criticised for this, his friends said he had a brain, and it was wasted here - he should be in the War Office! James Thirsk in *Bletchley Park: An Inmate's Story* tells a different version, where the routine task is potato peeling! Elizabeth records both versions, and both are true - he hated paperwork, and he was not manually adept. It was not only once that his friends protested he was wasted in the ordinary army!

When he was recruited to MI8, in 1940, the work demanded a detached and logical approach (he was a chess-player), mathematical grasp, and an ability to 'think outside the box' - all qualities he had in abundance.

His first child Andrew was born in May 1940. When she was far advanced in pregnancy, Elizabeth left London to stay with Neil's parents in Cheltenham. Neil was working in Caxton Street, when one night during the blitz, she was talking to him on the phone, in his flat in Warwick Square. Over the phone, she could hear the whine of bombs falling. Then, in her words "there was a shattering noise, and a lot of scrabbling ...then Neil's voice came cheerfully over the wire, 'It's all right... I'm under the table...' "

*Cribs for Victory* takes up the story of Neil's life from enrolment in the London Scottish in 1939 through recruitment to the War Office in 1940 to the end of his involvement in Intelligence in 1946.

Throughout this period, he was often separated from Elizabeth, and wrote her the lively and observant letters, of which excerpts are included in this book. By necessity, they do not include anything about his secret work. But they throw light on the wartime culture, the people, the places, the personalities, and the effort of the long struggle.

The letters cease when they were together in Harpenden (late 1940 to summer 1941), and again in Beaumanor (summer 1941 to autumn 1942 during which time a daughter, Jocelyn, was born) when they had an idyllic cottage in Woodhouse Eaves, and finally ended when they had a house in Fenny Stratford, Bletchley from spring 1944 till the end of 1946.

James Thirsk comments: "At Bletchley Neil had the reputation of being absent-minded. There was still a lot of his childhood lingering within, and at times, although having a friendly outgoing manner, he appeared to be living in a dream. All those who worked with him had a warm affection for Neil." He goes on to describe how Neil earned the nickname of "Wee Willie" at Bletchley, by bringing in candles when there was a power cut in the huts, like the *Wee Willie Winkie* of the nursery rhyme.

After the war was over, as he describes in *Cribs for Victory*, Neil took some jobs in journalism. The family moved to The Thatched House, Wateringbury, Kent where a fourth child, his youngest son, Godfrey, was born in September 1946. In October that year, there was a minor accident at home involving the third child, Roger (born 1944 in Cheltenham) who became critically ill and died in hospital, aged two and a half. This tragedy struck the family hard in the early post-war years.

Elizabeth began teaching and developed a career as a music critic. Neil returned to government employment in 1947 when he joined the Reference Division of the newly formed Central Office of Information. Elizabeth jokingly warned him "you will be there for life!" – and he was, working there for nearly 30 years until 1976.

In 1960, Neil and Elizabeth moved back to their roots in Gloucestershire, to a lovely old house near Painswick. Elizabeth taught Speech and Drama in Pates Junior School, Cheltenham, while Neil commuted to London, staying in digs during the week.

In Gloucestershire, he used his communication skills to help Elizabeth get her many novels published at last, and then joined with her to found in 1967 the Young Arts Centre of Cheltenham (YACC) – the first children's art centre in Britain. For twenty-three years they ran this pioneering creative charity, using Elizabeth's skills and imagination as a teacher, producer, author and costume and set designer, and Neil's good humour, time and energy and patient negotiating skills with authority. Children came, grew, and became young adults, and blossomed into creativity. One account by a young member (now a leading theatre producer) was given in the history of the YACC later published. An extract is quoted overleaf:

## HOT PURSUIT
by
Neil McArthur

There was in Cheltenham's fair town
A humble church hall, by renown
The haunt of an unruly band
Of players, artists, minstrels, and
Those elders who were educated
In guiding the uninitiated.
This building in which they were posted,
Blessed with so many assets, boasted
Stage dimensions of such span
They plunged in shame The Everyman.
So here the gallant company
Rehearsed 'Twelfth Night', a comedy:
Presiding over this gay caper,
A critic from the local paper
(Whose husband frequently was gone
To get the heating system on).

[Elizabeth's comments] 'This speaks for itself, but it also clearly spells out my poor, patient husband's role. When anything wanted doing, Neil did it. When anyone needed tackling, Neil did it. When finances wouldn't add up, Neil managed it.' "

[From: *The Young Arts Centre Cheltenham: The First Twenty Five Years* by Elizabeth and Neil Webster 1992]

When Neil retired, age 70, in 1976 from the Reference Division of the COI and from his Chairmanship of the COI Branch of the Institution of Professional Civil Servants he received many letters and accolades.

An extract is given below from a long letter of appreciation from Henry L. James, Director General of the Central Office of Information:

"Dear Neil,
How do you say au revoir to a personalized institution? In so many ways you are to me the I.P.C.S. - not just during my time at COI, which is rather less than six percent of your own, but as a fellow information officer for over more than a quarter of a century.
You must know that you have made a wholly personal and singular contribution to the evolution of COI and the Information Service as a whole. It is a thing we both believe in...

I think we can claim to have made a contribution to democratic understanding, and in the wider world to international understanding... I think with such mutual understanding COI as a community represents something of a microcosm of civilization. And for this you may claim considerable credit... I know you are due to retire on your 70th birthday on 7th November. As a statement of fact this is impeccable. As a statement of probability it is unlikely. That is the measure of your contribution."

From *Notes for a Valedictory Speech* by a colleague

"Neil Webster is seen by his colleagues in Reference Division as a truly civilized man: a man whose values are moral, cultural, intellectual – not at all those of the admass society; a man of moderation and steady enthusiasms, a man of profound courtesy who is not fastidious about superficial appearances. Absent-minded, untidy and a devil for losing unclassified papers, he is admired for his skill as a professional writer, for his amiable and charitable disposition and for his knowledge and wisdom. Schooled in the humanities, his approach to work and relationships is both humane and scientific. It is symbolic that he graduated from Oxford and later went on to do post-graduate work at Cambridge. He is an ideas man – his head in the heavens (maybe), his feet on the earth (more or less)."

In 1976 the Institution of Professional Civil Servants awarded Neil the N.E.C. (National Executive Committee) Special Award for Long Service.

The Foreword describes how, after retirement, he began writing *Cribs for Victory* and the events that ensued. In the late 1980s Neil's heart murmur finally caught up with him and he became ill and died in 1990. At his funeral in St Mary's Church, Painswick, the poem by John Donne, quoted at the beginning of this book, was read out – in recognition that the pursuit of truth was his lifelong endeavour.

His granddaughters have an enduring memory of him, while he was still well. When he once drove them over to Gloucester bus station to catch the coach to London, he entertained them while they waited in the cold by dancing the Scottish sword dance right there in the bus station!

# The War Letters

During research for Neil's biography these letters were discovered bundled together in their envelopes. They were never intended for publication but the more they were studied, the more it seemed that they should be published.

Of necessity they mention nothing about the secret work but they tell of the same sequence of events as that covered by *Cribs for Victory,* describing the settings and the personal experience of wartime and the characters encountered along the way. He wrote to 'Darling Betty', starting when Elizabeth was still his fiancée and going on through their marriage and the birth of their children, their enforced separations and their necessary arrangements for setting up home together in several locations. First they picture pre-war London, then the London Scottish battalion in camp, then wartime London, then the move to Harpenden and The Warren, then Beaumanor and lastly Bletchley.

Because they were in their envelopes it has been possible to construct a timeline and sources of letters and their destinations – facts not often in the letters themselves. The many personal and intimate passages about his wife, children and family have been omitted. The selection here is made on grounds of relevance to the text of *Cribs for Victory* and to the wartime contexts.

There are various gaps as stated in *About Neil Webster* either when Neil and Elizabeth were living together or when the letters were not pertinent. Wartime stringencies are very evident in the letters – most are written in pencil on scraps of paper varying from thin utility paper and pages torn from notebooks to postcards and hotel headed notepaper – and even one envelope containing no letter at all, and bearing a 3d postage-due stamp, but on the inside of the envelope a message reading 'No notepaper but much love'.

They are a marvellous resource, a treasure trove of immediacy, mostly very good humoured and occasionally showing the long strain of six weary years of war.

8 August 1939

*From London to Sidmouth, Devon where Elizabeth Heygate was on holiday*

'It's been a rather grey and mournful three days in London and your letter this morning was a great diversion. James* has gone. Mrs. M. is away so I'm all by myself, doing for myself. I don't like it...

Bank Holiday. Arrived home with 1s. 4d., no James, no Mrs. M. Tried to get credit at the delicatessen. But the girl who knows me wasn't there and the half-witted Greek wasn't helpful. So bought two eggs and lunched off same. Discovered that light had run out and radio wouldn't work... lady downstairs lent me ten bob.

Tuesday. Had phone calls from two designing females... Oh yes, there was a phone call for you – a young man called Alan with a slightly cockney accent. He said he's met you skating.

Wednesday. Went to a parade. Discovered I leave for camp Tuesday week. Drew a battle dress about four inches too big for me in every direction...

A not very satisfactory letter from Pete in Daytona [Florida] in which is raging one of the most comic opera political rumpuses of which I ever heard tell...'

[* *James Donald, the actor and film star, who was Neil's step-cousin and lifelong friend*]

30 Aug 1939

*From his camp at Catford*

'Well, well, well I afraid that now I've been cut off from the phone I've not been so good at getting in touch with you. But really it is hard here. You've seldom got time to get out a pencil and paper... and any spare time you do have you want for washing and sleep. Today, however, I have lots of time. I'm on guard. Two hours on and two hours off...

I proudly enclose three quid for you to buy yourself fun and fairings. If I keep it I should lose it or spend it on beer.

As for news: 1. We are still interned and working like a lot of 'bloody navvies' to quote the phrase that is on every man's lips. 2. I'm very well, have been excused heavy lifting by the M.O. and am enjoying the perfectly marvellous weather, the highly adequate food and the return to the comparative comfort of the palliasse. But I loathe a tin hat which I have to wear. 3. The chaps on a whole are a nice bunch, especially the socially less distinguished. The 'gentlemen' have a slight tendency to be like 'brother Ronald', who arrived two days ago - too sweet and smooth and cliquey. 4. I have absolutely nothing to do except fatigues and guard – unless I go on the Lewis guns which are, I gather, very noisy and very dangerous in war time. 5. I don't know when I can get to see you. You could, of course, come down to Eltham, take a bus to Unilever sports ground and then talk to me over the railings at the end of the Scottish lines – but if you do find me, I can't promise that half the battery won't turn up to have a word with you. 6. Odds and ends about the camp…the 'geography' is outside the night sentry's beat. So when I wander at night, I have to go through the whole rigmarole of: 'Who goes there?', 'Gunner Webster, going to bogs', 'Pass, friend'.

Everyone determined to be soldierly swears and grouses bravely…'


*Not dated but probably from Eltham, Kent in early Sept 1939*

'Thanks for your letter received the morning. Enclosed find cheque to cover things. I'll write Mama tonight to let her know my intentions and towards the end of the week, I'll try to get leave from the adjutant… Now, about the flat furniture. Would you prefer to store all you can't move into this flat Jack mentioned. Buy a Homefinder. That should give you an idea of prices.

I finished Eyeless in Gaza…and yesterday I played five games of billiards. So you see I'm not overworked. In fact I spend much of my time on the roof in the sun, where I am now – in blue overalls with a rug, a tin hat and a gas mask. Very restful and pleasant.

But I think I shall leave writing scandal, politics, literary criticism and psychology until I get a writing pencil instead of a drawing one…

So here's to seeing you soon in church, and till then and ever after, much love from Neil.'

*From Eltham, Kent. Postmarked 13 Sept 1939 9.30am but written the day before. The 13th Sept was the day of Neil's wedding to Elizabeth Marjorie Heygate.*

'A last note, Bets Darling, to Miss Heygate. As usual largely composed of requests and demands. I phoned Mama to try and pick up my driving licence from Handley Cross and I've made up the form and am returning it herewith. I think Middlesex Guildhall is the place to get it. But you can check. If you can get it (the licence), try and hire a small car in town. Herewith £7. 0s. 0d. to cover deposit and hire.

Well, love, that'll be all as I must catch a driver to post this. While we're in church we'll probably forget about the family and the lunch will certainly be funny and I hope brief. And don't tire yourself out flat hunting.

All my love, Neil'


22 September 1939

*From Catford*

'…We got back to Artillery House this afternoon [after his brief honeymoon]. The A.T.S. are still here doing cookhouse but they go tomorrow. A pity! They all cheered and waved their forks (they were eating) as I jumped down from the lorry. The colonel's secretary invents reasons for me to be alone with her (will I come in every night and black out the colonel's office). It must be my being a newly married man. Does it affect the men at your office that way? Can you explain the psychological mechanism? I've had two wedding presents – a quid from Eddie Dalton and two guineas (it makes me feel like a pro) from dear old Mrs. Campbell. How did you like my cookhouse sergeant on the phone? He's pleasant and nice to work for…'


*From Aberporth, Wales (Not dated but probably December 1939 or January 1940)*

Thank heavens, Darling, I have comfortable billets. It's the one redeeming feature in an otherwise pretty grim weekend.

The journey from Eltham to Whittands was ominously good. We

had a remarkably smooth and warm lorry journey to Paddington where we caught the 8.55 South Wales express… We were homey and civilized and comfortable and got to Whittands (some 250 miles) in about six hours. We got out into driving sleet and a sixty-mile an hour gale in which we had to unload kit and then leave it on the platform to get drenched while we waited fifty minutes for the Cardigan train in the ticket hall – I also tried the ladies' room, which was empty and had a fire, but came to the reluctant conclusion that that was letting down the regiment. On the Cardigan train we were eight or ten to a compartment with no corridor. It came on to snow and it took nearly four hours to cover the twenty miles to Cardigan. There, after more kit loading and stacking, we marched through the slush to await transport in the local pub. In about half an hour a lorry arrived and took us the twelve miles to Aberporth.

The accommodation provided for us was a large, draughty barn-like building with a wooden floor with shelves or tiers, each about six inches below the last. The three large iron stoves in it were rusty and unlit but full of coal. There was no kindling but I went and cadged some from a cottage and got our fire going, blew up my lilo, piled both my ground sheets, my greatcoats, my gas cape on top of my blankets and sleeping bag, wore my long woolly pants and a sweater and, along with the unit, spent a warm and comfortable night.

Yesterday was rather hell. I was first an ammunition number on a gun. To our surprise though our practice firing doesn't start till Tuesday, we have had to keep a look out for submarines. We had some heavy work uncovering and recovering the guns and then I was shifted to do a couple of hours spotting. The guns are on top of a three hundred foot cliff and catch the full brunt of the wind. But, thank heavens, there's a really big stove in the rest hut. By last night we were all pretty exhausted and looking forward to a hot meal and comfortable billets. The first we did not get. Cold salmon out of a tin was the cookhouse's miserable idea. But the billets I got. Jack Robertson, Murray Anderson, Richardson (the part-song enthusiast) and Kelby (a grand little tough old soldier) are billeted on Mrs Davies. I have a room to myself…

Today, after taking turns at half-hour intervals at submarine spotting I'm sitting by the fire listening to Kelby spinning army yarns…'

*Neil Webster, 1940*

SURNAME *WEBSTER*    INITIALS *M.L.*
ARMY No.    RANK *Gnr.*
REGT. OR CORPS *977aa Regt. R.a. T.a.*
SQDN., BTY., COY., etc.    *298*

# TERRITORIAL ARMY
# SOLDIER'S POCKET BOOK

*Neil and Elizabeth Webster, 1940*

*Neil with Andrew, Harpenden, June 1941*

*Neil with Joss and Andrew, Woodhouse Eaves, 1942*

*Burcote, Staplehall Road, Bletchley, June 1944*

*Bletchley, June 1944, family plus two friends*

*Bletchley Park staff, including members of Hut 6, in 1945.*

Sitting or kneeling (left-right): *Miss Iona Jay; Mrs Winifred Smith; Mrs Maureen Gentry-Kewley;* **Major Neil Webster***; Peggy Rawlings-Smith; Paul Coles; Major J. C. Monroe; Mary Groves; Major Edward Rushworth; Audrey Cocking.*

Standing (left-right): *Joan Watkins; Elizabeth Granger; Jean Davies; Jane Morris; Pat Downing; R.A. (Bob) Roseveare; Sheila Rawson; Harold Fletcher; Squadron Leader George Davis; RSM Asa Briggs; Molly Bruce; Pam Bevington; Jessie Proctor; Sheila Dunlop; Jean Proctor; Joyce Robinson; Major J. C. Manisty; Honour Pass; Daisy Genge; Gwen Thomas; Mrs H. M. Queening; Miss P. Hope Wallace.*

*Hut 6 Traffic Identification Section (TIS) at Bletchley Park.*
*© Crown Copyright. Used by kind permission of Director GCHQ.*

*SIXTA, Block D, Bletchley Park.*
*© Crown Copyright. Used by kind permission of Director GCHQ.*

*The intercept control room in Hut 6 at Bletchley Park, during WWII*

*Colossus, one of the two main codebreaking machines at Bletchley Park.*

*Typical envelope and scavenged notepaper*

TELEPHONE :
REGENT 7000 (40 LINES)
TELEGRAMS:
"UNTIPPABLE, PICCY, LONDON".
CODE:
WESTERN UNION.

REGENT PALACE HOTEL,
PICCADILLY CIRCUS,
LONDON, W.1.

*Tuesday*

*Excuse this amazing stationery. Only envelope I could find.*

*Elizabeth Webster ('Betty')*

*Elizabeth Webster with Andrew, London summer 1941*

*Hamish Blair- Cunynghame (left) and Edward Crankshaw*

*James Donald (left) with Alec Guinness in David Lean's film*
The Bridge Over The River Kwai

Form AB-47

UNITED STATES OF AMERICA
DEPARTMENT OF COMMERCE
AERONAUTICS BRANCH

## STUDENT PILOT'S LICENSE

Issued to **Neil Leslie Webster,**

Date issued **Febry. 22nd,** 19 **55**

DESCRIPTION OF STUDENT PILOT

Age **28**      Color of hair **Brown**

Weight **110**      Color of eyes **Brown**

Height **65"**

Remarks: **Qualified for Transport License.**

By authority of the Assistant Secretary of Commerce for Aeronautics.

Signed by *Rayl Green M.D.*

*Authorized Medical Examiner.*

This Student Pilot's Permit is not valid unless signed by an authorized Medical Examiner.

**This Certifies,** that the person whose name and description are given on this permit is registered with the Aeronautics Branch, Department of Commerce, as a Student Pilot, and is hereby authorized to operate licensed aircraft only while receiving flying instruction. The holder shall not be in command of aircraft carrying any other person and shall not carry cargo in licensed or unlicensed aircraft. The holder may make solo cross-country practice flights, but while away from home airport on such flights, shall not make landings on airports where flying meets or air races are in progress, or at airline terminals.

All provisions of the Air Commerce Regulations are made a part of the terms hereof as though written herein. The Regulations prohibit any but licensed transport pilots from giving instruction in licensed aircraft for hire.

Unless sooner suspended or revoked, this permit expires two (2) years from date of issuance as indicated above. It is not acceptable for a higher grade of license after nine (9) months.

This permit must be carried at all times while receiving instruction in or piloting licensed aircraft.

11—9884     (Student pilot's signature)

*Neil Leslie Webster*

*Neil Webster's pilot's licence and international driving licence*

This licence is not valid in Great Britain and Northern Ireland where a valid Driving Licence must be carried.

UNITED KINGDOM OF GREAT BRITAIN
AND NORTHERN IRELAND.

**103539**

INTERNATIONAL MOTOR TRAFFIC.

## INTERNATIONAL DRIVING PERMIT.

INTERNATIONAL CONVENTION OF
APRIL 24th, 1926.

ISSUE OF PERMIT.

Place **L O N D O N**   **1 AUG 1949**

Date **AUTOMOBILE ASSOCIATION**

*Gibson*

SECRETARY

† Signature of Authority or Signature of the Association empowered by the Authority and "visa" of the latter.

PARTICULARS CONCERNING THE DRIVER.

Surname     1

Other names     2

Place of birth     3

Date of birth     4

Home address     5

NOT VALID AFTER
3 1 JUL 1950 19

The Automobile Association.

*Neil Webster, 1940*

*Beaumanor Hall*

*Nymphs in the garden: Joss, Jill & Andrew. VE Day 1945*

*Sketch of Neil given at COI farewell party.*

23 February 1940

*From Aberporth, Wales while still on gun battery training*

'… Thanks for Le Temps, Le Jour and Le Petit Parisien. It's nice to know the French are not so hush hush about weather news as we are and that the French army are issued with a million pints of wine a day.

Today I'm a mess orderly which means I have the afternoon off save for one hour between 6.15 and 7.15 so I have lots of time to clean equipment.

… We've had an afternoon's firing. The noise was not too bad and we were quite good. No digs fixed up for you yet…'

4 March 1940

*From Wales*

'… A perfectly heavenly day, Darling, and it's a shame you can't be here. Still this afternoon, I couldn't have been with you. I'm sent to the 'manning station'. This 'manning' is a wonderful business. Two 3.2 mobiles are standing ready for action while the gunners lie in sunny sheltered nooks all over the cliffs snoozing, reading the Sunday Pictorial, and awaiting the call to arms. In the midst of a small group snoring louder than the rest stands the Identification Telescope, still pointing at courting couples on Pennlyn Beach, that so intrigued Gunner Webster. The group should be only two. But the reliefs have been too kind hearted to awaken the sleepers. So there's quite a concert now.

We've just had some mild excitement - sufficient to rouse the sleepers round the telescope. Two big Whitleys*, one right low over Aberporth village and another miles away west. Norman and I got it on the height finder but it was out of range. Now there is a school of porpoises and everyone is watching in turn. My do they jump…'

[* *Armstrong Whitworth Whitley bomber – a British aircraft. So hopefully they must have been practising!*]

11 May 1940

*To Elizabeth in the nursing home in Cheltenham. (Neil's first son Andrew had just been born).*

'Just a pencil scribble before I get planted in the office for the evening – on battery office phone. I rather wish I could go up to the guns and join the sandbagging fatigue on the extra Lewis guns which we are at last putting up. But I got this job instead.

I got your letter this morning. Am glad that you and Andrew continue to progress, that papa is so bouncy, that life 'passes by your window'.

About my trip to town – instead of sailors off a minesweeper, I had for companions some Scottish R.A.M.C. chaps… and the navigation instructor of the Stavaton R.A.F. school, a very pleasant man to talk to but slightly crippled and somehow a little too shy and too wise as cripples sometimes are.

I rang Beryl and told her briefly that you had had a son and you were all right.

I wish my transfer would come through…  it is too early yet to ask Captain Ken to ask his cousin to find out what's happening.

Get well quickly…'


12 May 1940

*From Dartford to the nursing home.*

'[*Lots of personal concerns*]… For the rest, I've done absolutely nothing since I came back. I've been taken off the course as there was no chance of my finishing it… No word has yet come through official channels about my transfer but that is not surprising.

Sandy Roger and Nigel Burgess are still here, also McKinnon, so things are not too dull and, of course, the war news has woken the site from its stagnation.

And, finally, love to Andrew…'

15 May 1940

*To the nursing home*

'… A very lovely day, Darling, and again very little to do. I've spent most of the day revising my little book on Calculus. I've also sat at the battery office phone while Sergeant Mollie Oakie had lunch and done two hours on the I. T. This morning everything was unusually rosy and everyone in the hut got out of bed the right side.

McKinnon while still half asleep had an amazing wisecracking bout with Nigel B. [*Burgess*]. Sandy Roger swept the room! I suppose the feeling that at last we may be in desperate action, all too soon, has stirred people up. I don't think myself they'll come yet. Hitler believes in concentration – one thing at a time. He'll only bomb England when he hopes to follow it up by invasion and gain a real military objective. Still no word of my transfer…'

17 May 1940

'Again, Darling, a lovely day with gold all over the gorse… First, how are you and Andrew?…

Of myself, no further word about my transfer although the officers all seem to think I'm going any day. I'm very well after quite a busy 24 hrs. I was on phones from 16 – 20 hrs, on the gun 20 – 22 hrs and from 03.45 to 06.15 and on I.T. from 10 till 12…'

19 May 1940

*From Dartford*

'God, what a time you've been having. [Elizabeth was having nursing problems with Andrew]… But, for God sake, if Andrew's starting to put on weight and you are beginning to get back to normal, with a safe well-paid job in store for me and with the codes and ciphers dept. probably moving to Cheltenham for a month (this is a pure guess but not an unlikely one) the only thing we have to worry about is poor old Holland (damn the bloody Belgians).

Last night, I slept in battery office and was kept awake all night by ridiculous phone messages about parachute troops. Not decent warnings that troops had landed at such-and-such a place but the same vague admonition to be on our guard coming in separately from all the civil and military authorities. Finally, I kept the light on and arranged the field and post office phones on chairs by the table on which I was sleeping so that I could reach them without getting up. After that, it was better.

McKinnon put his foot in it last night with that fool Carruthers. There was a practice turn out and everyone but Carruthers knew it was a practice. Carruthers tried to drive the non-duty men down into the shelters and was surprised when he met with passive resistance. Afterwards he rounded on McKinnon: 'Why didn't you say it was a practice?' McKinnon: 'I thought you must know, Sir, you were so calm.' Nothing more was said and Carruthers left.

Still no news of my transfer. On Friday, I'll tackle Ken...'


21 May 1940

'... I'm sorry Mum worries but I'm not surprised. Still, the news today is better. And thank God since Churchill came in, the news is more intelligible. Imagine having to hear of the present situation through the woollen mist of one of Chamberlain's pronouncements. Incidentally, as regards the defence of this site, the position has been much improved by two little boys flying their kites. These were taken for parachutes and before the mistake was discovered – had got 4 Lewis guns, 2 sub-machine guns, and 150 '303' rounds out of Vickers. (This is confidential to cheer you up), though the real cheering fact is that Hitler won't bomb until his attack on Britain is ready. By that time I should be sitting over a first-class air-raid shelter and entitled to go there. No further word about the transfer...'


22 May 1940

*From Sidcup, Kent*

'To my intense surprise, darling, I find myself back at Cray tonight. I was shaken gently by the shoulder at 5.30 a.m. and instructed to have my kit up by 9.00, up and stacked on the guard hut veranda.

Of course, we didn't move till 12.00 and, of course, we had lunch at 11.15 before we left, after I'd packed my knife, fork and spoon with the kit that went ahead.

Cray was looking lovely, buttercups in the meadows and white blossom on the trees. We took over from '299' at one o'clock and at once the snags began to appear.

B and C sections are manning Cray, leaving A and D at Dartford. We found that for the afternoon we had just two I.T. men, myself and Jones. I had four solid hours on the command post with innumerable odd planes popping about and messages from the dugout to keep me on the alert. Till tomorrow night we're three which means two hours on, four off. Then Butt comes back. In the meantime, I expect my summons to London any minute. Which will leave them in the soup again.

So far as I can see, we must get another draft immediately…

Incidentally, Jack Robertson's little problem has been solved in the silliest possible way. The army, finding him indispensable as a soldier, refused to release him to the Evening News. They have now, however, relented so far as to compromise. They are giving him a pip and he is to edit the Southern Command magazine. He seems quite pleased!…

I shall leave you to join in with the gaities of the Cray Institute. Nigel is playing jazz. Bill Tweddle is playing ping-pong with a little plump, red-haired, snub-nosed, red hot dumpling of an A.T. There is another ping-pong table and I might cut in now but I'm tired. So I'll try to get an hour's rest until I go on at ten.

But, My! Is this institute nice with flowers on all the tables and a new stage at the end…'


23 May 1940

*From Kent*


'…Today, I've received three from you…

Not much news here. Things are pretty quiet, but yesterday with a south wind we could hear the gunfire in France ever so faintly. I don't hear it today. So perhaps we really have moved forward. I don't think Hitler could raid this country without a terrific loss of bombers so he daren't risk it unless he can follow up at once.

I'm starting a little song against the N.A.A.F.I. to please the Y.M.C.A. [*where he is staying*]

We're the friends of the British army
We're the boys at the N.A.A.F.I. bar
It's treason to say we look barmy
Or hint that our grub's below par
We don't pamper your constitutions
We don't care a damn how you're fed
Like all well entrenched institutions
We'll be here when you're bloody well dead

That's all so far as I've forgotten the next bit of Nigel's tune...'

2 June 1940

*To Elizabeth at Neil's parents home in Cheltenham. He had now been transferred to London*

'Well, Angel, here is a slight pause in activities during which I can write to you. I've had a fairly easy morning on the whole and have had time to make out more forms about kit allowance etc.

My dinner at the Saville last night was not an unqualified joy though it was very nice. Blair-Cunningham [*sic*]* is an excellent though over earnest young man. He gave me a very good dinner and we had a nice talk. Later we were joined by Col. Stratton and a friend and had another nice talk. That was fine for Col. Stratton and his friend who are over 50. But Cunningham [sic]* should have more devil in him at 29.

I'm now at 37a Churton St. Suddenly Capt. Wishart came in and said would I go on the night shift 12 – 8 and have this afternoon and the whole of tomorrow off.

… This uniform business I've managed rather well I think. Moss Bros. have made my uniform fit me nicely. I got everything except for camp kit and overcoat for just under £20, which leaves me £10 clear and I discovered a shop where I can get ready-made shoes that really fitted. And shoes (2 pairs) and socks and two pairs of summer pyjamas and a very good raincoat that fits me properly are included in the £20. Altogether I think I have done very well and look lovely!

I'm getting into the work now and learning quite a lot of German in the process...'

[* *Blair-Cunynghame*]

5 June 1940

*From London. He complains about how to use his evenings after a long day's work and goes on the say:*

'… I saw an excellent picture A Window in London and had most interesting talks with the long-jawed bloke from the N.A.A.F.I. who gave me his card, Charlie Muller, London's Harmonica Virtuoso, a huge Canadian sailor who told me that some American millionaires had offered untold gold for the proven bumping-off of Hitler and that three men had set out three months ago. I had besides a brief and devastating chat with an elderly tart who said in a refined Cockney voice ' Dear Boy, I want you to come home with me. I have a lovely flat quite close by and I have a very beautiful body'. I replied in the same vein ' It sounds most charming but can't we make it another evening?' and ducked hastily into a brightly-lit milk bar.

Leicester Sq was thick with 'birds' hunting the B.E.F. [*British Expeditionary Force*]. It is at times like these that I regret the poor quality of the London 'bird' and the high price of all other London amusements… If ever an army deserved a real soldiers' welcome, this one does. They've shown that while the German and the Frenchman on the whole are less good fighters than their fathers, the young English are perhaps better. And, God, do they look impressive! Both the ones you see and on the newsreels. There has never been as sharp a propaganda weapon in the hands of Britain as those newsreels leaving Dunkirk and earlier Boulogne. Thank heavens they got at least 75% away…'

18 June 1940

*From London*

'Alack and alas the day, it looks as if our tidy arrangements about Andrew's christening may be disturbed by rude military exigencies. The roster is to be changed. Tomorrow when I discover how, I may make an appeal to Colonel Str. [*Stratton*] and fix a definite date when I can get down to Cheltenham.

Last night I met an enormous and pleasant medical student in the delicatessen. We had a couple of beers and went to a newsflash and walked on the embankment. Today, I had a nice morning chat with a Rhodesian lieutenant of tank. Life is not bad.

But times are bad, Darling, and the fifth column are working at high pressure and still we are only half awake to the danger. Otherwise things are good with me. I'm back off shift work and back on the regular research work... But, oh God, how long and bitter this struggle is going to be and how bankrupt this country will become...'


3 July 1940

*From London enclosed in a piece of fancy notepaper from the Regents Palace Hotel, Piccadilly Circus*

'Excuse this amazing stationery but only envelope I could find.

Well, it was not exactly a hell of a party but it was quite fun. The Antelope, the Wellington and some spot where you have dancing till midnight and are supposed to pay a shilling to get in but we didn't. Hugh Burden and his sister Anna, Evers Austin – I think that was his name, a tiresome young woman called Lucille, Donald and myself were the central core of the party. Both girls had pashes on Donald who is quite sweet but needs sparking. Donald had no place to go so I put him up in 37a Churton St. We talked till 2.45 before going to bed...

As for yourself, are you starting to feel heartier? What about the magnum opus? Have you started it?

My news is nil. A quiet day without Captain W. [*Wishart*]. Had expensive lunch at a smart place with the whole gang from the office. Rather dull. Great confabs and plans between junior officers.

Seen nothing of Tony or James or anyone we know...'


4 July 1940

*From London*

'... My evening with Tony [*Pirie*] and his weird friends was quite amusing. Tony was in very agreeable form but unshaven and the change from my somewhat tight-lipped brother officers was pleasant.

Du reste, the office is quite interesting. If I mind my step and all goes well, I can start something really useful and become a key man in it. Besides I'm back with B.C. [*Blair Cunynghame*] who has a lazy, inventive, high-geared mind. Given to astonishing bursts of application and sceptical boredom in between. Such a relief after Captain W's patient, verbose bragging...'

29 July 1940

*From London*

'I walked up to 298 Battery's Hyde Park camp last night. Rather a disappointment...

Today has been a completely infuriating day – lots to do and no chance of doing it. Everyone important away, and the people on routine jobs with strict orders from the absent bigwigs not to let the routine work get behind for anything. And there's an entirely new routine starting tomorrow under my supervision and I've had no chance to explain it or discuss it with any of the people who are to carry it out. My, oh my! ...

A lovely day today but I'm a little cross. There's nowhere near here where one can get a good cheap lunch or a sandwich on a Sunday and that spoiled my lunch interval. Besides, I'm furious at the makeshift way we are forced to work.

By the way, Blair-Cunningham told me the finest example of departmentalism. A foreign friend of his that had been passed by the W.O. [*War Office*] for work in the secret service was arrested in the general blanket arrest and was half way to Australia before any protest could be made. He was one of those who had been fighting in the Pioneer corps.

The German planes are over every night but seem to do nothing. What I wonder are they playing at. Of course, there are setting up the Balkans but these isolated bombers are very odd...'

25 October 1940

*From Harpenden*

'... Well, here at last is a moment suited to writing to you. The Spinney is somehow impossible – the sitting rooms are too heavy and hot and the bedrooms too dim and cold but my hour at the Warren waiting as duty officer for the Home Guard to turn up ought to be just right.

Just me and Corporal McIntosh in the house and he's busy setting up the H.G.'s beds on chairs and stealing shovelfuls of my fire to light the one in the kitchen, which serves as a guard-room. He has just reminded me that we forgot to wear our gas masks from 17.15 to 17.45. Thank God for small mercies.

Now the phone's gone! Just the operator at R- - d wanting to know if he should send on the letters tonight or tomorrow morning. Who'd read them tonight, damn him?

So now to continue my letter by the dying fire in this fine drawing room with the green carpet and the faded brown and silver covers to the too plentiful armchairs and the sofa on which are scattered my chess set and writing case and the revolver I've borrowed from Chris.

This is the room we use as a clubroom. In one corner stands a bureau converted to cocktail cabinet with special wireless set dials and panel – a mere façade – built into the top as a decoration.

The real music – at the moment someone's particularly boring Faust - is provided by Freda's gaudy little Philco portable.

Add mauve curtains with wavy green and red stripes, wavy like cardiographs, covering the windows and the glass door to the loggia. Also a large gilt mirror and in a gilt frame a naked lady rather too stout and with a Victorian hairstyle sitting on a bank of a wooded stream. And you have a rather unfavourable impression of this really solid and comfortable room.

I've told you over the phone of my interview with the goofy young woman who wishes to work for us, and of my contact with the local movers. But I wish you could have seen me career round Harpenden on Iva's bicycle with the green saddle to these good people. And the superb self control of stray O.R.'s [*Other Ranks*] when asked the way by an officer on a lady's bike. Here come the H.G. the same old Corporal, thank God. Nothing to show him.

But they had no milk for their tea! They'd run out and after McKintosh and I had searched the house to see if the computers had left some in a cupboard, and found none, the H.G. Corporal asked leave to go down to R.C. to beg some. Well, he can go – but I feel I should stay till he comes back…'

[*Letters cease till July 1941 because Neil and Elizabeth were living together during this period in Harpenden*]

30 July 1941

*From Harpenden and Beaumanor recording the move*

'… [*Sunday*] From tomorrow, love, my address is Beaumanor, Woodhouse, Leics. Just name and rank, no unit. Things will be pretty chaotic at first, the blackout's not done and the private exchange not started. But I expect it will be quite fun. But I think we must have a billiard table. Otherwise there'll be some terribly dreary evenings…

[*Monday*] At the moment all is chaos. But in the capable hands of S.Q.M.S. Smith order is beginning to appear and everything is getting stowed on four 3-ton lorries.

I feel I need not interfere and am quietly continuing my letter. It's now 16.30 hours. In about an hour I must get on a lorry and set forth. We won't be there till about 21.00 hours and then we must unpack. God, what a game.

[*Tuesday*] Here we are at dear old Beaumanor. The lorry was late yesterday and I didn't get to the house until 11.05. I had quantities of tomato and pilchard sandwiches and coffee on the way and dinner and two whiskies when I arrived. But I stood the shock remarkably well.

This place lacks an adequate blackout and is in the most hideous bad taste. But the grounds are pleasant and we are comfortable. Colonel Thompson, thank God, is not coming till tomorrow. Hamish and Wesley, the adjutant, have gone to London. Philip's still on the road from the Warren. I am officer commanding Central Party and a beautiful peace reigns, and I have restored equanimity to the N.C.O.'s by converting guard duty and office cleaning into a combined duty called 'picket'.

22 August 1941

*From Beaumanor*

'…The hotel didn't run to a writing room so I'm now scribbling in the ante-room after a fairly quiet busy day. Hamish, you gather, is away for a few days and our only worry is Heller, who shows a tendency to project his vivid imagination into the work.

By the way he told me the perfect Heller story. We were discussing the suggestion of his going to London to work under Crankshaw.

(Joanie V. may be going too, a frightful complication, but I did not mention this). The chief drawback I foresaw was the probable hail of bombs. 'Oh bombs,' said Heller with familiar contempt. 'I attract the damn things, but I'm not dead yet. I was only ten feet from the one on the Café de Paris.'

'Good God,' I said 'What happened?' It seems he was having a backshi weekend with a married girlfriend and had taken her to the Café. He had just leaned forward to drool in her ear, when the hit came. His amorous advance saved both their lives as it put a pillar between him and the bomb while he covered her. Moreover the falling balcony only just missed him and hit the back of the chair in which he had been sitting. Even with the protection of the pillar, he was blown across the room. He felt a sharp pain in his ears and saw a thundering flash, but the explosion was too violent to permit any sound sensation. But he and the girl were unhurt but covered with black ash and blood. This was just as well as it would have been awkward to explain to the husband that his wife had had to stay in London when she wasn't supposed to be there at all. What a perversion of human values. A queer card, Heller…

Today, I had a good game of tennis with Chris [*Wills*]. But somehow without you to share them my pleasures are rather dim. Must not let myself get flat though as the place in Hamish's absence depends on my vitality to a quite considerable extent…'

7 September 1941

*From Beaumanor*

'… Well, darling, here's the good moment to write to you. I'm duty officer and everyone else is going to church. Everyone apparently except Wishart and Wesley who are pacing the lawn together. More trouble I fear.

The usual rows have been going and Hamish is pretty tired. I bear up pretty well but am getting a trifle bored – not with the work – but with the people. For all he's a bit bogus Heller is the best companion. Hamish just won't get off shop and the others are too young. Still, after a couple of day's leave I may see all things including BM society more rosily… Wishart's just been in, lost the Yale keys to his private safe, most agitated. Heller, who is I think a Jew and an agnostic – he's told me he's a Jew by birth – is sitting in a corner of the officer's room reading a large worn book.

Well, here they all come back to work. I must start playing with a beautiful spider's web of coloured wool. [*Possibly a reference to his log readers' star diagrams*]

22 September 1941

*From Beaumanor*

'... Philip Lewis and Horace West are in here with me. They came in to work but in fact are not doing anything except gossip and consult the army list.

I am in mufti having refused to change back after tennis. The Colonel did not mind but just beamed at me like a mooncalf. I felt a bit annoyed at his still being there though as I'd counted on being alone in the room when you rang up...

My arrangements for the fortnight are complete except for the car and I expect I can fix that.

Major Haig has told me I can use the truck to collect your and Andrew's personal effects from the station so we should manage.

The woman that is coming to do for us in the mornings is very nice indeed. The evening cook I don't like so much but she's harmless I suppose. We'll see if she can cook.

I'm still a bit under the weather from Sergeant's mess do. They do do themselves much better than we do. It takes Sergeants to buy a good mahogany table for 6s 6d, to have a plentiful supply of eggs and milk, two people competing to lend them pianos, and to train a concrete mixer to make some of the best puff pastry I've ever tasted...

Life of course is smoother without Hamish. I hope there's not too much explosion when he returns... Rodney Bax is going to start harmony classes. I wonder how good he is. In any case it might be fun for you to attend if it didn't make him too shy. His class will all be very musical and will include Hannery who says he wants to start again from the beginning, and Major Hughes who can read and appreciate a classical score but has never had a theoretical training. There will also be Russian and Economics classes and debates, play reading and whist drives. Shall we teach Andrew [*Neil's baby son*] Russian to fit him for the new era?

Love, Darling. I must away.'

29 October 1941

*From Beaumanor*

> year old schoolmaster, who wore a perpetually dazed look. I hope he's not as dumb or as insecure as he seemed. He's been out East & confided to us, that though he wasn't much good with a shot-gun, he was hotstuff at hitting sleeping crocodiles with a rifle and that he had lots of crocodile skin suitcases. A mistake, when he looks like a lizard, anyway.

I've just been showing around the work a sleepy fat lizard-like fifty-year-old schoolmaster who wore a perpetually dazed look. I hope he's not as dumb or insecure as he seemed. He's been out East and confided to us, that though he wasn't much good with a shot-gun, he was hot stuff at hitting sleeping crocodiles with a rifle and that he had lots of crocodile skin suitcases. A mistake, when he looks like a lizard anyway.

Jennie Beer and I seem to be making a success of this report* which is becoming quite a pivot of the organization. I hope the damn thing doesn't make me late on Friday. I must arrange incidentally to be duty officer on Thursday and orderly officer, Wednesday. That means I can get home late on Thursday nights and only spend Wednesday nights away…'

[* *This was probably 'The Beaumanor Weekly' forerunner of 'The SIXTA Weekly'*]

*At this time letters cease until October 1942 as Neil and Elizabeth were living together during this period in Woodhouse Eaves. In summer 1942 Neil went to Bletchley while Elizabeth and family stayed in Woodhouse Eaves.*

25 October 1942

*From Bletchley to the The Old Cottage, Woodhouse Eaves, Leics.*

'…After looking for a Trades and Commercial [*Street directory - Neil was looking for accommodation*] unsuccessfully in the Post Office I found one in the pub and am going down this evening to copy down some names.

After seeing you Monday I went to a bad Humphrey Bogart spy story called Across the Pacific (though they never got further than Panama)… Milne (Bob) has returned from his leave very sprightly. He went to see Heartbreak House, Love for Love, and Hedda Garbler of which he warmly recommends the last. That, and A Month in the Country do seem worth seeing, if I can.

Have now had dinner and am sitting in office listening to chat and shop mixed. Stout little Paddy Bradshaw, dumpy bow-legged 4 ft 6ins A.T.S. officer with a slight beard but none the less quite charming arguing with the encyclopaedic Rushworth…

It's rather pleasant sitting here writing to you and helping Basil Malabre, the D.O., to answer occasional queries…

Surely this is the right milieu. It's full of the left handed, the slightly stammering, the eccentric mannered, the haywire and academic of every age and sex…

*Not dated but from Bletchley to Woodhouse Eaves. On the back of the envelope is written:* 'Dear Spooner, could you or Mrs H. drop this on Betty'

' The weather is fine and brisk. My billet [56 Eaton Avenue, Bletchley] is comfortable and clean and Mrs Blare is nothing if not attentive. Work at the Park is going not too badly and there are lots of new faces and a good sprinkling of comely wenches…'

[*An inserted letter of personal discussion*] '…When I have the blues, it's mostly liver. Don't you think that if we wrote sour grapes when we felt sour grapes and plain rice pudding when we want plain rice pudding, we'd still have as much trifle as is pleasant and wholesome…I, more than most, am possessed of a spirit that waxes and wanes like a flame burning, now high, now low…

Anyway, that we should worry! Amid the blood and toil and sweat, I kill Germans by doing interesting, academic work. I spend my off days with my two engaging children dressed in attractive clothes made for them by my pretty wife who is also a good cook.

Besides I get staff-captain's pay and you have domestic help. That we should worry! Hell!'

4 April 1943

*From Bletchley to Woodhouse Eaves.*

'…Nothing to tell you very much. Mrs Blare has discoloured the inside of her lip – I have it on her authority. The doctor says its bootleg lipstick. But she's not satisfied. My does she rattle on about it.

The office goes on as usual – no change in the routine of work and backchat.

Let's talk now about the future, what we want out of life and how we propose to get it.

First of all, of course, we want a good home for Andrew and Jocelyn [Neil's daughter] until they are ten, or say, twelve… Until then it comes first.

Then we want to work at something that feels worthwhile and we can do as well, or better, than most people.

Next we want to grow in wisdom and favour with God and man, and for our children to grow in stature, as well.

Then we want the graces of life – art, culture, friendship, witty company, fun and adventure. Of course, all of these things dovetail but that is the order I put them…

Oh well, enough of my prosing. You will notice my style got more priggish as my pencil got blunter – a curious psychological point…

By the way, about the last two headings, if we get the first two, we may assume that these will be added to us. Or don't you agree?'

11 April 1943

*From Bletchely to Woodhouse Eaves. The Americans joined the unit in that year. The letter begins with an apology for having spent time being depressed about the future.*

'…The main thing that was the matter with me was that I was

tired. It's shown in my work since I got back. I must go to bed early for a few nights. And think, as far as I can, not about what I'm going to do. That is what the small men do and it gets you nowhere but about post-war tasks and standards, the proper function of publicity and its mechanics, the role of the intellectual.

I think Transatlantic is rather a heavy effort. It is, I think, the first acute symptom of the decay of Americanism as a mode of self-expression. I mean that America produced men whose vivid diction grew more from the life around them than from literature. Their written word had a direct Elizabethan impact. Self-conscious pedantic Americanism will surely kill that gift…It's hopeless, anyway, to make English men like America by explaining it to them in this patient way. A sudden and violent conversion is needed…

We moved yesterday, having moved the office furniture the night before. The new quarters are palatial but draughty and I have to go miles to see people. Still I share a corner with three others instead of eight…'

### Undated from Bletchley

' I'm sitting tonight in Mrs B's sitting room after listening to the news (quite good). Too lazy to do my blackout and light my fire for just an hour. I ought to turn in early if I'm to get all the tickets and catch the morning train to town…

The train picture books are sold out in Bletchley, so I'll look in London tomorrow…

Chief news in Bletchley is 'old Greene is fine'. 'Old Greene' is a furniture dealer whose father went bankrupt time after time but persevered until he got rich. 'Old Greene' had some sheds at the back with stored furniture and these are what have gone. The possibilities are endless…

Friday night. Yesterday, after finishing my lecture at Hampstead, I rang up the Ministry of Labour and managed to get hold of Reggie and fix a lunch date at the Bristol Grill. He was a wreck. Sallower and more sunken-eyed than ever, hoarse from the congestion in his lung, and weary from endless office responsibility and family care. Charming and witty as ever and the same liberal, critical mind. But for all the drink – and he would drink double whiskies to my single – it was clearly an effort to be gay. But it was somehow very comforting to talk to him again…back to dinner with Reggie at La Coquille. He'd had the hell of an afternoon with a farmer J.P. from

Kent who thought he had a scheme for making gypsies do National Service. The man, said Reggie, was a caricature and his ideas of the shotgun type. The interview lasted two hours and had to be conducted in a bellow.

His private news I've told you but he said some interesting things. The Ministry of Security brains trust does exist. Some of his friends are on it and very bored as they have to sit all alone by themselves and think. Heavenly I should say. They are just on the point of exposing a really big medical exemption racket depending on fake X-rays...He said he's never known Andrew's birthday, so I gave it to him...'


1 July 1943

*From Bletchley*


'Yesterday, love, I had quite a good day. I got my report finished early and biked out and lay in the sun and had lunch in The Swan at Fenny. A good lunch and good fun. I was reading Orwell's Road to Wigan Pier and listening to ITMA [*It's That Man Again - the famous radio comedy with Tommy Handley*] as I ate. A good book and a great programme. Much appreciated by the blearily regal old dame opposite and her two Cheltenham gentleman friends...

Orwell's quite a lad and his book's good but depressing. Not his account of slum conditions – those one knew and they can be remedied. But his acceptance of the fact that the ordered world which may succeed our muddled one, will be ugly, characterless and, above all things, dull. At least he doesn't say we can do nothing about it but that we can only hope to mitigate the dullness slightly...

Wednesday. I'm writing this now in James's flat. Here's James's news in brief. Korda's offered him a fantastic contract: a £100,000 or so, spaced over eight years of eight month's work a year. He's wondering a little as the first part offered him is bad. But in view of the four free months, I feel he should take it...

I saw A Month in the Country, a good play but they take it too slowly and Redgrave is getting soft...'

7 Sept 1943
*From Bletchley*

'The rich food at The Fountain was a bit much for me and today I'm going on bread and butter and feeling rather limp… I've been looking like the gloomy uncle all day working silently to the background of Cockney anecdote, French and Italian gossip and girlish laughter (Mayfair style) which is the background noise of the registration room…'

3 November 1943
*From Bletchley*

'…Today I came in to find the Park full of the smell of coffee in the sun-warmed autumn air. And I felt better at once. Reminded me of Paris and New York and idle days.

I'm writing in the evening in the office, and the American Bob Britton is opposite me reading the paper. We're going to work a while and then going to the dance with Rodney [*Bax*] and Christine [*Brooke-Rose*]…

Bob Britton used to be assistant programme director of N.B.C. I ought, I suppose, to keep up with him but he's a queer shy bloke, terribly attractive in a studious but apparently lackadaisical style. He strums dreamy jazz very pleasantly. I must introduce him to James Donald, 'the rising star of radio, stage and screen'.

I've not done any more about houses in past few days but Morna did do one thing. She rang up Alan Lane's wife* who is an old bosom pal about houses in Staines…'

[**Allen Lane, the publisher, who founded Penguin Books*]

1 December 1943
*Postcard from Bletchley*

'I'm so sorry your flu is giving trouble. Be careful and do what the doctor and nurse tell you.

I plan to come and see tomorrow night. Try and be better by then.

I remain completely robust and feel rather a pig about it.

Glad the children are better'

8 December 1943

*From Bletchley*

'I heard, love, from Jo that you were getting better...poor you, last week – with a fever and choking and pregnant besides. Jo says you should be quite yourself by the time I come down.

Last night I went to a film Millions like Us, which was authentic but rather wet. Then to the dance, the free hop, where I danced with a thin girl in a grey flannel dress who was a dance teacher and danced quite well. She was however otherwise colourless, in fact, rather wet in much the same way the film was.

For the rest I still escape the flu. The epidemic seems to be tailing off a bit in the Park. So many have had it.

Don't overdo it with the children until you're quite better.'


1 January 1944

*From Bletchley*

'Well, I had the flu, though only a very mild go. Two days of a temperature. This morning it was normal so I got up and went out to phone and see if there was an emergency, which there wasn't. The Park doctor called and told me to stay away till Monday which seems excessive. I intend to drop in for a couple of hours this afternoon and see that everything is shipshape... Meantime I've been reading the Christmas Carol.

You cannot imagine how attentive the Blares have been [his landlady] bringing more tea and toast and cocoa and hot water bottles at all hours. Putting a fire in my bedroom, getting me yesterday a special invalid lunch of fish and rice pudding and ringing up the Park to let them know how I was going on...'


*7 March 1944*

*From Bletchley to the nursing home in Cheltenham where Roger, Neil's second son had been born.*

'I'm lingering at the billet after breakfast to write you this note. Most improper but I was working till very late last night...

I bought a Penguin symposium of 'post-war' speeches. In it was Acland's maiden speech, an attack on capitalism. Interesting among the optimists and euphemists. You would, I think, dislike it.

Have you got the nanny?… I've seen two more horrid houses in Bletchley to be auctioned March 15th…'

14 March 1944

*From Bletchley*

'Can you deal with this? [*Missing enclosure*] I think it would be a nice idea but where do we put her. I've talked to James D [*Donald*] who is alive and in an awful Priestley play. He was very drifty and vague on the phone. Is that the effect of the army?

You and I have been asked to a dance Wednesday week. That's Roy being a bit vague, I expect…'

28 March 1944

*From Bletchley*

'Darling, I'm sitting in the billet and listening to the news and feeling rather glum. It's the aftermath of flu which make me feel the long years of my own inefficacy. I've written to Nigel [*Burgess*] but again I can't find his address and I haven't a pen, which is the conventional weapon for some business letters I might write. I've done one thing anyway – tidied the letters in my draw. I must go to bed early as I want to work at speed tomorrow. I have a big job and I want to get through it by 5 p.m. when I catch a train to Tring where I play chess against the R.A.F. If I can, I'll get back on Wednesday night; if not, on Thursday teatime and go back by the 10.55 a.m. on Friday. I must be in the Park for the night of March 31st.

There is, of course, nothing much to tell you. The long fight goes on. We too fight in our own way and for all its softness, we sometimes wish it were another way. Hence this sense of futility…'

*In April 1944 Neil together with his family moved in to a house in Fenny Stratford and the letters cease.*

# Part III

# The Fusion Room Confusion

Clipped with the *Cribs for Victory* typescript were various letters and a paper. These are included here.

Before the book was stopped, as described in the Foreword, these papers were kept by Neil, possibly with the intent to make use of them in a final version. What they show is the considerable confusion that existed in the 1980s, forty years on, about the role of SIXTA and the Fusion Room.

To decide whether to include them we had first to find out who they were from. Some of the letters had clear sources but two had only undecipherable signatures: these were the letter with the paper and the letter to Ralph Bennett, both from the same person. This, from the content, was clearly someone in Hut 3. At first we thought, from the mention of Rodney Bax and his first wife Christine Brooke Rose, it might be from Oeser, Head of 3L as Christine worked in 3L and in *Cribs for Victory* it is mentioned that Rodney was seconded to Hut 3. But in the end tracking the author down involved a trip to the British Library to view the Electoral Register for 1985 to search for the occupants of the address on the top of the letter. We discovered that a Major Roger Howard and Jean Howard were living there. Checking the Role of Honour on the BP web site, we found no Major Howard, but did find Jean Howard, née Alington, who was in Hut 3. All the letters then made sense – Robin Denniston copied his letter to her; Jean's letter to Ralph mentions the Almássy papers (Jean was involved in translating Almassy's intercepted and decoded signals from the Western Desert while he was serving as a spymaster for General Rommel, and later was involved in advising on the film *The English Patient* supposedly based on Almássy's life, though later still she dissociated herself from this version) and all the mentions of Rodney were understandable.

The paper *Preparation for D-Day Programme* was prepared for a proposed TV programme but was not included in the programme in the end. It describes the confusion about roles: 'I pointed out to Bill Milward that we had been looking for information on MI8/SIXTA/Fusion Room/Central Party/Bolitho's angels. If that multi-headed hydra (which in my dictionary is a Southern constellation!) was unable to stay in one place, or to know what it called itself for more than a few months, who were we to be able to keep up?'

The paper goes on to try to establish the roles and quotes Neil Webster's draft paper and then various other responses from BP people. General Gadd comments, 'The control of interception was never properly managed in my view and was effective only because a few people like Gordon [Welchman], and later Oscar [Oeser] and 3L, studied the problems. There were both technical and security aspects that added to the difficulties. Hamish B.C., Neil Webster and Philip Lewis (whom you don't mention) were the key players on the T.A. side. SIXTA was a belated effort to rationalise matters and was my particular baby.'

Towards the end of the paper are Welchman's comments. He agrees with Jean that 'each person, working flat out, thought they knew everything, whereas each person has tunnel vision'. He then makes it more apparent that this was so by disagreeing with everything everyone else has said. He misreads Neil's description of the task of the intercept operators, which is astonishing since *Cribs for Victory* is all about logs and the intelligence they yield. And as for his comment 'I have no recollection of the Fusion Room', he must have been having a bad day! He is grumpy about it and everything else in the paper! He had moved to the USA at this time and had been criticised by GCHQ and US authorities for the publication of *The Hut 6 Story* and subsequent papers. However what he does say positively is that 'the Central Party deserves to have its praises sung, but not for T.A'. It does seem there was a terminology problem between all of them.

Ralph Bennett's letter to Neil throws more light on interception policy, and the perceived roles of Hut 3, Hut 6, and the Central Party in determining what were priorities for the listening posts. But even here it is evident that each group valued their own role highest. However, Ralph says he now realizes 'that cribs had to be the number one priority (otherwise there might be no intelligence at all)'.

The other letters are self explanatory.

FROM ~~THE PRESIDENT~~
R. F. BENNETT

MAGDALENE COLLEGE
CAMBRIDGE
CB3 OAG

TELEPHONE 61543

18 January 1983

Dear Mr Webster,

Thank you very much for your letter and for letting me have a sight of your most interesting paper. I have taken copies of some of the pages which are most useful to me (I hope this is all right?) and return the original herewith.

Taken together, letter and paper have rectified what I might not otherwise have recognised as an error of focus. To me - until I read your paper and reconsidered what Stuart had said in the light of it - interception policy almost self-evidently must have been guided by the desire to provide us in Hut 3 with the best possible intelligence. Now I realise and understand better (what of course I knew at the time but had allowed to slip into the back of my mind) that cribs had to be the No 1 priority (otherwise there might be no intelligence at all) and that the 'search for the stars' was a legitimate end in itself. I am most grateful for being thus made to get my proportions right.

To do so is not to solve my original problem, as you remark, though it does go some way towards doing so. Stuart had, of course, confirmed my memory that we and they (Hut 6) had regular liaison about intercept policy, but he stops short - just as you do - of saying that the two of us decided what should be listened to and what should not. I am now clear that three elements at least were fed into the decision-making process (if there really was one)- Hut 3, Hut 6 and your Central Party - but I have yet to discover whether anyone ever refereed their meeting and decided exactly what to do. Perhaps in the end the intercept stations took ad hoc decisions after taking all these needs into account: an odd conclusion, if true, but one which somehow fits the Bletchley atmosphere.

Anyway, thank you very much for the help you have given me; I am most grateful for it.

Yours sincerely,

*Ralph Bennett*

*Ralph Bennett to Neil Webster*

Telephone:

East Horsley
  3 7 7 9
                                   Camilla House,
                                   Forest Road,
                                   East Horsley,
                                   Leatherhead,
                                   Surrey KT24-5-BB

                                   9th February,
                                     1983.

Dear Mr. Webster

      Thank you very much indeed for your kind
letter of January the 26th.   I am sorry that
I have not replied earlier but I am not very
well at present.   Of course I would be absolutely
delighted to read your memoir and, if you would be
good enough to lend it to me, all I can say is that
I would treat it with the greatest possible care
and, of course, I would not make any reference to
it in writing without your permission.

                            Yours sincerely,

                            Ronald Lewin

*Ronald Lewin to Neil Webster*

```
Telephone:

East Horsley
   3 7 7 9                          Camilla House,
                                    Forest Road,
                                    East Horsley,
                                    Leatherhead,
                                    Surrey KT24-5-BB

                                    22nd April, 1983.
```

Dear Webster

     I am returning now the memoir which you kindly sent me, and am sorry that I've been so long about it, but I think I explained that I have to take things rather slowly. I thought that you would not mind if I had a copy made for my files, or if I sent it on to Stuart Milner-Barry, who is a great friend of mine (as is Gordon Welchman). Incidentally, have you read Gordon's book which came out last year entitled 'The Hut Six Story', and published by Allen Lane? He goes into the initial break-through into Enigma in great detail.

     There is just one point. It's all a long time ago, but I wonder whether you can put a date on our acquisition of the various German call-sign books, etc. In forming a picture, it would clearly be useful to fit them in chronologically.

Yours sincerely,

Ronald Lewin

Ronald Lewin

Enclosure

*Ronald Lewin to Neil Webster*

**BRITISH BROADCASTING CORPORATION**

KENSINGTON HOUSE  RICHMOND WAY  LONDON W14 0AX

TELEPHONE 01-743 1272   TELEX: 265781

TELEGRAMS AND CABLES : TELECASTS LONDON TELEX

16th March 1984

Neil Webster, Esq.,
Turnstone House,
Greenhouse Lane,
Painswick,
Gloucestershire

Dear Mr. Webster,

Thank you for your letters and your enclosures.

I'm editing at the moment but I'll be in touch after I've had a chance to assess all the information about Bletchley.

Yours sincerely,

(Roy Davies)
Producer, Music and Arts, Television

*Roy Davies to Neil Webster*

# Oxford University Press
## Walton Street, Oxford OX2 6DP
Telephone 0865 56767 Cables CLARENDON PRESS OXFORD Telex 837330
ACADEMIC AND GENERAL DIVISION  Publisher R. A. DENNISTON

RAD/am                                          4 March 1985

Dear Mr. Webster,

      I was talking the other day with Jean Howard about the possibility
of a book that might be written about the Y Service.  You may know that
we had a contract with Ronald Lewin to tackle such a book, but he died
when the idea was in its infancy.  Since then I have not amassed much
new material but I do have his file, and I know about your own excellent
contribution.  It occurred to both Jean and me that you might yourself
be the right author.  If you are at all interested please let me know
and we could talk further.

                                        Yours sincerely,

                                        Robin Denniston

N. Webster Esq.,
Tunstone House,
Green House Lane,
Fenswick,
Glos.

cc: Jean Howard

*Robin Denniston to Neil Webster*

May 17th 1985

Dear Ralph,

You will remember that the most substantial recollections on 'Y' came from Neil Webster, so will not be surprised that Robin Denniston routed Ronald's remnants to him. Neil came to luncheon with me today; the first time I recall meeting him, though we must have met at Christine and Rodney's wedding. He is a charming man, with a nice sense of the absurd.

Neil does not believe that a book including the Far East would be practical by now, and has other reservations. He has not yet discussed his findings with Robin. ( who seems akin to the Robin I miss so badly from my garden at Churt, always hopping on and off the spade and into the bushes.... worse I cannot always read his letters, and if they have enclosures these are missing).

I cannot imagine how Ronald Lewin would have tackled the subject, Even the language between individual sections became obscure.  No doubt it would have been a fascinating soufflé, but there are security problems to circumnavigate. We all knew that Gordon had trouble with NSA on the Hut 6 book. I did not know, until Neil told me, that our own authorities had been equally annoyed by it.

Did you know about, or have you been asked to the School of East European Slavonic Studies, who are said to be having a Yugoslav jamboree on May 29th, which is a first confrontation of ideas. I'm told that Biber, Barker, Pavlowitch and Beloff, are among the 'combatants'. Michael Foot has been asked too.  I'm supposed to be sailing down the French coast in Rustler, but if it is snowing I might jack out and try to get in on the act. (The Evening Standard said that there was trouble at the SEESS. To do with Djilas' son.)

How kind of you to collect the Almasy references, I should be very grateful to have them.

With best wishes to you both

from

*Jean Howard to Ralph Bennett*

**11 KNIGHTSBRIDGE COURT**
**SLOANE STREET**
**LONDON S.W. 1.**
01 - 245 9976

May 24th 1985

Dear Neil,

It was good to see you. Here is a copy of the letter I wrote to Ralph... it answers his queries about who was going to write the book, without in any way committing you to doing so.

Since seeing you I have had a letter from Christine; her mother died. She sounds very lost. I will tell her we met after all these years, and that will amuse her.

A Professor Winks from Yale has written a long letter asking if I remember a man called Colonel Ted Hilles? He says he ran the Americans at Bletchley. Hut 3 do not remember him, we thought Telford Taylor was in charge of them, although of course he was away a great deal overseas. Was Hilles one of yours?

Another up to date copy of the D-Day research. I think I sent you one that was incomplete. My wordprocessor had broken down.

Shall be interested to know what you decide to do. Please keep in touch.

Yours ever

*Jean Howard to Neil Webster*

# Preparations for D-Day Programme

by Jean Howard

Asked by Roy Davies of BBC *Chronicle* fame, what preparations GC&CS made for D-Day, I said that we had made arrangements to cover the frequencies in the Cherbourg Peninsula which had up to then only produced practice messages. Until their land lines were bombed there had been little from the area on the cipher of 7th Army, which we were going to call Duck. There would be the German Air Force cipher Red, which also covered liaison with the German Army.

Curiously, on discussing this with other members of Hut 3, there was a complete blank over a section I remembered as MI8, with which I had liaised on double banking of particular frequencies, and who could tell from the call signs of an unsigned   message, who sent it and to whom it was addressed.

It occurred to me that I should get hold of Rodney Bax (a High Court judge). I was sure that he had something to do with MI8. After 40 Years it was fun to see him again, we arranged to sail our yacht to his Channel Island to eat lobsters. He had worked in the Fusion Room and on the Watch. He asked me to get in touch with his first wife Professor Christine Brooke Rose. She was now working in Paris.

Within a few days I heard that he had died.  This was a great shock, he was younger than any of us. I wrote to tell Christine what had happened, and she came over to spend two days with us... slowly we pieced together what had happened forty years before: she remembered clearly that the Fusion Room had read the intercept logs, and traced units using individual call signs from operators chat, and 'Y' Service intelligence as described in Aileen Clayton's book *The Enemy is Listening*.  We had captured the Bird and Elephant books which helped us to decode the call signs.  She gave me the names of the four Fusion Room officers who worked on the watch, collaborating with the Military and Air Advisers.  They could usually tell by the call signs and /or Fist (radio finger print) where unsigned messages originated.

Christine told me to write to Telford Taylor, to get the American point of view.

Telford Taylor wrote a lively letter which answered my question as to when the Americans had joined us: He came over in April or May 1943 and the others followed to Hut 6 and Hut 3 in mid-summer. He did not enlarge on the MI8/SIXTA problem.

John Monroe told me that, at the beginning, there was a section of MI8 working at Beaumanor, on the Y intercepts, and log reading the intercepts. This moved to B.P. in 1942 to Block D where it was called SIXTA. A Major Wills took over from Hamish Blair Cunynghame (I remembered a Colonel Gadd as being part of or controlling that set up, but no-one else seems to). This is also covered to some extent in Gordon Welchman's *Hut Six Story*.

Monroe said that of course they would have worked on the practice messages coming up from the Cherbourg peninsula, Lautstaerke Funf etc.

I asked Stuart Milner-Barry whether I had got this right? That Bletchley preparations for D-Day included the coverage of frequencies likely to throw up German Army and Luftwaffe Enigma, in the event of our having disrupted the landlines, by bombing? That we knew the right frequencies from the intercept logs and the 'Y' service, before we had read a single enciphered German Army message from the Invasion area? We had always had some LW Red traffic from the Cherbourg Peninsula.

Milner-Barry agreed with the above paragraph, and sent me a fascinating 30 page article by Neil Webster, who had originally sent it to Ronald Lewin. Having not yet had an answer from Neil Webster himself I should treat it as confidential, however it is full of absolute gems and confirms that the task of Bolitho's Angels was to break the call sign system used by the German air force:

Neil Webster explained:

"that the radio communications of the German Armed forces were based on a star system. Control had no call sign. It called the outstation by using the same call sign which the outstation used to call control. Usually each star was allocated one or two frequencies and these frequencies would stay for long periods. The frequency was therefore an important factor in identifying a star.

"The communications between the stations and the German stars were in Morse code and consisted of message transmissions, most of which were in cipher or code and operators chat (keying, calling, notice and receipt of messages, queries, checks, cancellations etc.), which was mainly in the international Q Code used for brevity, not security, by most Morse senders throughout the world.

"British operators monitoring these communications at the intercept stations had first to write down every message on a message pad and, as soon as it was completed, hand it for despatch to the cryptographers at Bletchley. Secondly they had to record all operators chat and the preambles of messages in a log or as the Americans called it, a chatter sheet. The logs were handed over to intelligence officers at the intercept station who compiled from them a daily report of the frequencies and stars heard. These reports formed a basis of the attempted analysis of the call sign system"

29th February I had a telephone call from Neil Webster explaining that he had contacted Roy Davies. He added that all codes and ciphers could be transmitted on the stars. Not just Enigma. Groups according to areas. That the logs were sent up from Beaumanor about two hours after the decodes, on motor bicycles. (These I remember well as roaring up to the Hut). Of course by the time of D-Day Hut 6 had its own T/A, and Watch. Re-encodements were easier to spot on logs. Before D-Day there were new transmissions, and new settings, some unbroken. There was a big volume after D-Day. Central Party working from D/F retransmissions etc. Potential cribs were given 7 times cover. (This would not have applied to unbroken D-Day ciphers).

Bill Milward gave me a detailed breakdown of what other people were doing at that time. He was in 3A:

"3A and the opposite number 3M consisted of advisers to the Watch and a headquarters element responsible for oversight of air and military intelligence production respectively.

"At the relevant times Terry Leatham was head of 3M, Alan Pryce Jones his deputy. Correspondingly on the air side were Jim Rose and Peter Calvocoressi. I have no recollection of any special briefing of watch and advisers before D-Day. It may well have been considered unnecessary. We were at full operational readiness, had been for years, and we all knew what was coming. It could however be that the HQ of 3M and 3A were 'bigoted'. Certainly once the attack was launched Pryce Jones kept the watch in touch with progress.

"Interception must have been closely involved, but I never found out at Bletchley who controlled intercepts, if anybody. Control is normally hooked on to traffic analysis (log reading, general search, call signs, frequencies, schedules, network identification/recovery etc. You are right about SIXTA. T/A was originally done at Beaumanor in support of interception and presumably in Hut 6 in support of crypt. The Beaumanor party was moved to Bletchley (in 1942?) and combined with the Hut 6 element as SIXTA. MI8 at WO furnished the fixed intercept stations and oversaw mobile 'Y' in the army. The Beaumanor bit of Sixta will have come from M18 (T/A needs lots of bodies). There was a useful liaison officer from SIXTA in Hut 3. Was he your George Crawford?"

N.B. Bill does not remember the three Fusion Room Officers who worked on the watch, or that there were special efforts to cover the still unbroken and unused ciphers liable to come up after the Invasion. Was anyone in Hut 6 bigoted? Were they equally involved in covering the German 15th Army area in the Pas de Calais?

March 1st I pointed out to Bill Milward that we had been looking for information on MI8/SIXTA/Fusion Room/Central Party/Bolitho's angels. If that multi-headed Hydra, which in my dictionary is also a southern constellation(!), was unable to stay in one place, or to know what it called itself for more than a few months, who were we to be able to keep up?

A letter from George Crawford dated March 4th fills in some more of the puzzle:

"1) I joined BP in May 1940 as a Sapper in Colman's section. Our job was to keep a 24 hour watch on the frequencies and call signs used by different German units. When I arrived several breaks had already taken place, and they were looking for specific crib messages, also well known active and apparently important frequencies. The frequencies used by particular stations a) varied by German inefficiency or b) were changed by orders from above from time to time.

2) Once breaking was a regular occurrence, the decoding section in Hut 6 began to fall rapidly into arrears because of the time taken in changing machine settings as each Watch came in and changed the instructions of the previous Watch.

3) This was why 3L was set up. To give priorities to the decoding room and elsewhere.

"I cannot remember the job of the Fusion Room in all this, but one thing is quite clear that from the earliest days interception was closely organised to keep a watch on all frequencies of importance for cryptography (where letter perfection was needed) or intelligence... often with 3 or 4 machines on the most important messages: and to search out new frequencies, whenever they were changed. My recollection was that Colman's section continued until the end, as our contact with the intercept stations, so presumably the Fusion Room laid on what was needed through them... with 3L advising on the importance and urgency of messages already passed and decoded.

He added: "the extraordinary thing is that it worked so well and, so far as I can remember, with very little bloody-mindedness. With all the tensions and trouble of the war what a marvellous place BP was with lots of splendid and able colleagues and a great devotion to duty (and secrecy). In parenthesis I weep for what has been done for GCHQ.

A further letter from Stuart Milner-Barry says on March 13th:

"...it makes me deplore the stuffiness of the authorities in refusing me access to the sketch of Hut 6 which I recorded just before I left BP.... No, I didn't spot anything wrong, but I am astonished to find out how much I didn't know, of what was going on. But I WAS bigoted about D-Day certainly."

In July I contacted General Gadd... too late for the programme which in the event used none of this report... he said:

"The control of interception was never properly managed in my view, and was effective only because a few people like Gordon and later Oscar and 3L studied the problems. There were both technical and security aspects which added to the difficulties. Hamish B-C, Neil Webster and Philip Lewis, whom you don't mention, were the key figures on the T/A side. SIXTA was a belated effort to rationalise matters and was my particular baby.

"I congratulate you on your achievement in unravelling the mystery as you have done, and I'm sorry that it did not become a programme".

Robin Denniston was going to USA to visit Gordon Welchman, so I sent Gordon a copy of this paper. This was part of his reply dated July 22nd:

"It is indeed true, as you say, that 'each individual, working flat out, thought that they knew everything, whereas each individual has tunnel vision.'"

"It is quite extraordinary that almost all the information you were given was wrong, or at least misleading. I wish we could talk.

"The key people in the management of interception were Commander Ellingworth, and Wing Commander Shepherd.

"In 1939, when I had started to analyse Enigma traffic, I established a close working relationship with Ellingworth in Chatham. Early in 1940 I had a 24- hour intercept control activity under Colman, which kept in continual telephone contact with Ellingworth's duty officers. Then the big RAF station at Chicksands, which you do not mention, got going, Wing Commander Shepherd was very willing to learn from Ellingworth and from Colman. It was not long before Colman's team was working just as smoothly with the duty officers at Chicksands as they were with the Chatham ones. (pp.149-150 *Hut Six Story*) Note that the RAF ran a training school, that Ellingworth moved to Beaumanor, that he and Shepherd ran subsidiary stations to get diversified reception, and that special aerials were needed to pull in distant signals from Africa, the Balkans, and the Russian Front. I don't believe that Oscar Oeser understood all this, and I doubt if General Gadd did.

"You were greatly misled over T/A or Traffic Analysis, and Radio Intelligence which is very different. Throughout the war the analysis of Enigma traffic on which Hut 3 depended was handled in Hut 6, using the Traffic Register, that I initiated on my first visit to Chatham. (p56) Nothing else would have been fast enough.

The Central Party, when it moved to BP. from Beaumanor under Philip Lewis, was not housed in Block D. They were in a wooden hut, which I believe was Hut 5, but am not sure. But there was an outfit in Hut 3, under Lithgow, which I did not mention in my book. Lithgow was in charge of a Y group in France, and was sent to BP after Dunkirk. He somehow established a place in Hut 3, and managed to gain promotion by increasing the number of his subordinates. With help from Travis I managed to prevent his attempts to take over a part of the well co-ordinated Enigma activity. I could never see that he was doing anything worthwhile, but I have a suspicion that the 'Fusion Officers attached to the Hut 3 Watch' were his men.

"The Central Party was very different, and it deserves to have its praises sung, but not for T/A. I cannot go into my association with this group, which started in a small way in London (p.95). They and I realised in those early days that our ability to predict the call signs that would be used by the units subscribing to a particular radio net could be of great value to the intercept stations, to Hut 6 and to Hut 3 (pp.124, 153, 159).

"The appointment of Oscar Oeser is mentioned in my p 124. It was the result of my approach to the newly arrived Group Captain Jones. People in Hut 3 had no idea of what really mattered. Indeed they all had tunnel vision. I wanted someone in Hut 3 who would be able to grasp the overall picture.

"Although I liked him as a friend, Oeser was a great disappointment. He failed to grasp the whole picture:- the problems of interception - traffic analysis - log reading - radio intelligence. He concentrated, as you confirm, on priorities for the bombes. Which was a small part of the overall picture. I have an uneasy feeling that my old friend Milner-Barry never grasped it either.

"I am utterly puzzled by the terminology. I have no recollection of the 'Fusion Room'.

"I think you were misinformed about the control station of a German star network having no call sign. One of the great advantages was that, when the units involved were moving, any of the stations could take over the control function. You were also misinformed about the difficulty the Germans found in keeping a star active when it was not needed for passing traffic... a once a day exercise was inadequate.

"I am surprised that Neil Webster was so misleading, but maybe he never got to an intercept station. The FIRST TASK of British interceptors was not to 'write down every message on a message pad'. Messages were often rare, but the chit chat was always important, revealing all the call signs of a unit, and sometimes other information too, such as evidence of a retransmission.

He went on to say that Peter Calvocoressi had the best appreciation of the importance of interception, and that Ronald Lewin achieved a realistic picture. Hinsley, while doing a good overall job is shockingly wrong in his account of the first year at BP and the value of the Polish contribution.

"I could go on for hours, but must stop. Your letter has given me many ideas on what I must emphasize in my new little book, for it seems to me that the preparations for D-Day depended heavily on what was achieved in the first year at BP.

"I would like to send you a copy of my first draft and will be most grateful for your opinion on whether or not I have answered some of your questions.

"A great pity you did not contact Harold Fletcher and Reg Parker, who would have been a good substitute for Colman.

"Sorry to say that in my opinion George Crawford never understood."

AMEN

# From Fusion To SIXTA

The previous chapter showed the confusion and conflicting memories about fusion and SIXTA that were prevalent around the mid 1980s when my father was trying to get his book published. The correspondence included there shows many of the key players saying widely differing things.

Since that time much has been released into the public domain including now my father's book, which tells a very clear story. Preparing this book for publication has been a journey of discovery for me involving many hours in the National Archives at Kew, much delving into difficult subjects and the learning of many new facts about my father's life, including the existence of his wartime letters. My most recent discovery is that *The SIXTA History* (HW 43/63) still 'retained by the department' and not accessible to the public (see Foreword) is, in fact, the history my father was responsible for preparing as mentioned at the end of *Cribs for Victory*.

However, a great deal about fusion and SIXTA *has* been released. What follows is drawn from papers on the web, from the Archives and from James Thirsk's *Bletchley Park: An Inmate's Story*. These sources will have to serve until *The SIXTA History* is released. They foreshadow the theme reiterated at the end of *Cribs for Victory:* "I stressed then as I have now, that radio intelligence and cryptography must work closely together – so closely that they are practically one."

*Cribs for Victory* relates the story of the practical contribution made by the Central Party, with its fusion room, its log readers, and its idiosyncratic and lateral thinking brain-power, to the whole cryptographic and intelligence effort during WWII. It is particularly detailed with regard to liaison between the Y Service and the cryptographers in Hut 6 (my father's own role) and the technology of the regular breaking of Enigma. It doesn't dwell on the organisational changes that brought the Central Party, as SIXTA right into the heart of the German army-air Enigma complex at Bletchley Park.

When he was transferred to Intelligence in May 1940, my father found himself not, as he expected, with the code-breakers, but with radio intelligence in No.6 Intelligence School, which was being set up by MI8 (a branch of the War Office) to study enemy communications systems. This role would prove to be of central importance. The picture of enemy communications – who was saying what to whom and where – that was built up by the unit over time, when taken together with decoded messages, gradually enabled them to build up the whole German order of battle.

In the beginning, as he describes, there were three of them: Hamish Blair-Cunynghame, Chris Wills and himself. My father was the most senior, and at first in charge, but as he relates, soon ceded the role to Hamish. They were together for much of the war, but Hamish left in summer 1943, while my father stayed right till the end. The three of them first were set to breaking the call sign system of the German Air Force. They started studying logs, and then hiring and training log-readers, and then teaching the log-readers to draw 'star' network diagrams, and when Crankshaw saw these and put them together with what he knew from decodes, the concept of fusion was born.

From this small start the group ended up playing a critical central role in the heart of Bletchley Park – in an extraordinarily successful example of inter-service and military/civilian cooperation: the wartime collaboration between radio traffic analysts (War Office), and the intelligence officers and cryptanalysts at Bletchley (Foreign Office).

As *Cribs for Victory* relates, there had been another branch of No 6 I.S. already in Bletchley right from the beginning. This was the Special Liaison Party (S.L.P.) in Hut 3, under Lithgow. When the Central Party moved to Bletchley in May 1942, they absorbed this unit, as related in *Cribs for Victory* – but not at first. It was not until November 1943 that they moved into a new hut, and amalgamation was complete.

There is a document in the National Archives called *Dossier on SIXTA* (HW 50/66). This consists of pages of handwritten notes – names, times, and events covering the history, the evolution from MI8 and 6 I.S. to the Central Party and S.L.P., and the move of the Central Party from Beaumanor to Bletchley. It adds some discussion here and there, mainly to validate the facts, and notes that Crankshaw was brought in to study the amalgamation, and plan it, and then was appointed as head of the newly born SIXTA. There is a piece summarising SIXTA claims, of aid to Cryptography and to Intelligence, which bears close comparison with the more detailed account given in *Cribs for Victory*. There is also a set of notes on the 'W.T.I.

Controversy' about W.T.I. (Wireless Telegraphy Intelligence) versus traffic analysis, which ends with a piece marked 'Travis's Last Word' resolving the difficulty. "The basis of all SIGINT work is the same, namely that there are 3 partners inextricably interlocked, Interception, Traffic Analysis, and Cryptography whose function is to produce intelligence and to present that intelligence in a useful form to those who need it. Traffic Analysis – a name which covers much of what used to be called WTI..."

But the best, most readable record of the birth of SIXTA in the National Archives was written by Frank Birch, who was head of the naval section (Hut 4) from June 1941. After the war he was appointed chief of the historical section by GCHQ and then compiled an internal history, which is quoted below. References on each page show that much of his description of the birth of SIXTA is drawn from *The SIXTA History*.

In *A History of British Sigint Vol II 1942 – 1945* by Frank Birch (HW 43/2) p. 480 he describes the task faced by Travis taking over from Denniston in Feb 1942:

> "The original design of the Service side of GC&CS had expressed the simple principle of one Service, one Section, but in the course of building, so many contradictory ideas and anomalous make-shifts had been introduced that the resulting edifice was a hybrid monstrosity in keeping with nothing but the architecture of Bletchley Park mansion itself" (A humorous note is given below: 'so remarkable was the structure that no diagram of the organisation was officially issued until 1944. The best of many attempts to draft one is marked MOST SECRET, Most Misleading and Most Inaccurate'!)
>
> But built it had been, and D.D. (S) [Deputy Director Services i.e. Travis] was to find it difficult to modify – more especially that part of it which gave him most concern, the German army-air Enigma complex made up of Hut 6, Hut 3 and No. 6 I.S."

This complex posed a problem of organisation. "For one thing, its three components served a common purpose but not a common master" and again, "Hut 3 (Intelligence) was all of a piece; so, too was Hut 6 (Cryptanalysis); and both were at Bletchley Park. But the third component 6 I.S. (Traffic Analysis) was, when D.D.(S) took over, still in two pieces; one, the main body, at the military strategic Y Station at Beaumanor, the other, the 'Special Liaison Party' (S.L.P.) at Bletchley Park [in Hut 3]. To complicate matters further, a great deal of traffic analysis was also being done, in aid of cover control and crib spotting, in Hut 6, and a great deal in Hut 3, and not only by S.L.P."

He describes how the concentration of the whole of 6 I.S. in Bletchley Park had been mooted as early as 1940 and was increasingly desired by all parties throughout 1941 (even by Hut 6 which though at first hostile, became strongly in support of the idea). But it was not until the spring of 1942 that Bletchley could provide office space for the extra 100 personnel and the War Office a hostel for the A.T.S, so that the move could be made.

Even after the move was made in May 1942, and the whole of 6 I.S. were at BP, they were not united. "There was S.L.P in Hut 3 concentrating on decrypts and there was Central Party (CP) as the Beaumanor contingent was called, concentrating on logs."

As he describes, S.L.P continued to relate to Hut 3, and CP gravitated towards Hut 6, with which it was amalgamated in December. "Instead of rationalisation of traffic analysis CP and S.L.P were drifting further apart" and "misunderstandings marred the efficiency of the work"

The remedy was obvious - amalgamation. But this was not effected until October 1943 "and then only as a result of pressure from W.T.C. and of the completion of a new block of offices". The newly amalgamated unit began to function in late 1943 and was named SIXTA in February 1944. "Indeed from one point of view 6 I.S. had been reconstituted under a new name and under new management, but from another it appeared that for the first time a continuous T.A. process was made possible."

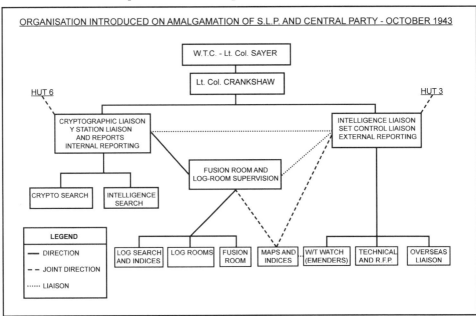

*Courtesy of the National Archives*

A diagram of the new structure shows the FUSION ROOM supervision at the very heart of it, with log-readers and fusion sector officers below, and Hut 6 and Hut 3 links on each side, and over it all Crankshaw, and above him Sayer.

Birch ends with the following: "Such was the tortuous evolution of this complicated organization. The product of uncoordinated historical growth rather than rational planning, it was marred by duplication in work, over-elaboration in procedure and extravagance in staffing. It is also on record that it lacked technical knowledge concerning sites, receivers and aerials, and experience of communications in general. Nevertheless, clumsy and wasteful as it was, it worked. All the defects mentioned ... might have been remedied if cover control had been the commitment of a single unit. I.C. (I) indeed advocated the creation of such a Section, independent alike of Hut 6 and Hut 3 and SIXTA. But this solution of the problem was practically impossible without the union of cryptanalysis, intelligence and traffic analysis under a common head. And that is just what was lacking in the army-air Enigma complex."

And that is just what my father was recommending in *Cribs for Victory*.

A contemporary account of the role of fusion in SIXTA was given by an American officer Lieutenant Robert G. Nunn Jr. who worked in the Fusion Room in SIXTA and was in charge of traffic from the Western Front Army at the time of the invasion. Entitled *Critical Observations on German Traffic Analysis in SIXTA*, the original document is in The American National Archives. It was reformatted and released by Tony Sale on his website *Codesandciphers* in November 2003. It gives the early history of fusion (somewhat inaccurately; Nunn admits it was based on hearsay, since he wasn't there until 1943) and goes on to say "The Beaumanor group was moved to B.P. largely as a result of the vision and energies of Blair Conynghame [*sic*] and Welchman. An organisation called 6 I.I. was grafted on to Hut 6 with Lithgow at the head, Gadd in charge of the original B.P. 'source' group and Blair Conynghame [*sic*] in charge of log reading and fusion. Under Blair Conynghame [*sic*] the proform method of log reading, a more liberal but still limited application of source in fusion process, a routine search for re-encipherments, in short the beginnings of the basic processes of T.A. – by SIXTA as it now is, was accomplished"

He remarks about this stage in the process that "Unification was at first painful, and at first avoided because it meant a radical reorganisation in which habits of work would have to be changed." He describes how Blair-

Cunynghame was called to Africa in summer 1943 and Major Lewis took his place, with Gadd still in charge of the 'source' side of T.A., and when in October Lithgow left for London, Col. Crankshaw took his place. "The lingering organisational division between Gadd (traffic readers, Source Bureau, Liaison Department and MI8 Watch) and Lewis (log reading, D/F [direction finding] and fusion) was finally broken down. With the moral support of Welchman, 'SIXTA' was formed and in November 1943 Lewis assumed command, the nominal connection with Hut 6 was severed although through the efforts of Major Webster, Capt Rushworth and Fusion Room sector officers, operational intimacy continued to grow. Traffic readers moved into the Fusion Room and the basic fusion process of reading traffic in its signals context was begun. The Source Bureau, Liaison Dept and MI8 Watch – in short, Hut 3 – began to rely on and in fact applaud the efforts of log reading and fusion. Hut 6 (Cryptography), Hut 3 (Intelligence) and SIXTA (TA) became operationally unified... The parts became a whole."

He goes on to say: "Thus, at the present point in history the integration of T.A., Cryptography and Intelligence no longer appears to be a proposition needing proof, but rather is a basic proposition which may be taken as the criterion of sound policy and efficient organisation."

A much more recent description of the Fusion Room and the birth of SIXTA in 1943 is given in *Bletchley Park: An Inmates Story*, published in 2008:

"The Fusion Room became the central part of SIXTA. By collecting information from the logs provided by the intercept stations it was able to construct the complete wartime picture of the enemy order of battle. It supplied information which enabled Major Morrison to build up his famous war map ... Hut 3 intelligence officers frequently consulted the Fusion Room on intelligence matters. It was also able to help the cryptanalysts of Hut 6 by providing information about call signs and frequencies and repeats of messages. A weekly publication THE SIXTA SUMMARY was circulated to sections of Huts 3 and 6."

It goes on to describe the Fusion Room senior officers "Working in senior positions in the Fusion Room were three men whose jobs included close liaison with the cryptanalysts of Hut 6 and the interpreters of intelligence in Hut 3. The phrase 'lateral thinking' only came into the language when Edward De Bono wrote of two methods of thought – vertical and lateral. The latter may be described as a method of seeking solutions of difficult problems by ignoring the orthodox logical approach and arriving at solutions from different angles. These three men who practised such methods all held the rank of army major. They were Freddie Edwards and Neil Webster ('Willie') ... and Edward Rushworth..." Freddie Edwards was a brilliant eccentric, a lively friend of my parents at Bletchley and, as *Cribs for Victory* describes, my father shared a desk with Edward Rushworth ('Rush') – Rushworth as Liaison with Intelligence in Hut 3, my father as Liaison with Cryptography in Hut 6.

# Glossary

ABWEHR, THE
Literally meaning defence - the German military intelligence and information gathering organisation from 1921 to 1944.

BLISTS
Lists of cipher settings with their preambles and the call signs and frequencies of the stations passing them, for each setting concerned.

BLITZKREIG
The military strategy of lightning breakthrough spearheaded by massed tanks. The Germans had developed this concept to include close air support by dive bombers and co-ordination of operations by a comprehensive radio network linking formations at all levels.

BLUE
Code name for the German Enigma practice key.

BOLITHO'S ANGELS
The band of bright, well-connected women recruited by Captain Hector Bolitho in Caxton St and used for top secret work from then on.

BOMBE
An electrical machine for testing rapidly all combinations and positions of the rotors to find those consistent with information supplied on a menu based on a crib (i.e. an informed guess of the clear text of a message).

BREAK
A decipherment of an encrypted message or system, or to decipher such a message or system.

BROWN
The code name for the key of the German experimental signals regiment.

CALL SIGN
The identifying label used by each separate unit of the German army or airforce when sending or receiving traffic. This consisted of three jumbled symbols (either letters or numbers) changed daily according to a fixed programme laid out in a call-sign book.

## CALL SIGN BOOK
A book containing thousands of call signs arranged in hundreds of columns and rows from which a station could select its correct call sign for the day.

## CHATTER SHEET
An American name for a log used in listening stations to record all information and operators chat and preambles.

## CRASH
A letter going to itself in an attempted decipherment, which in Enigma is not allowed. For instance, if a crib of forty letters could be fitted without a crash, there was a strong presumption that it was the right clear text and a correct setting.

## CRIB
A short piece of enciphered text where the meaning is either known or can be guessed, which allows the whole cipher to be broken. Cribs might be stereotyped addresses and signatures sent at regular times of day or repetitious content of routine reports such as 'Nothing to report' or repeats or re-encodements which were strong cribs.

## CROSS-PLUGGING
In an Enigma machine setting pairs of letters were cross-plugged so that the entry and exit points of each pair of letters to and from the scrambler were interchanged. There are some 40 million million ways of doing this.

## DAISY CHAIN
In an attempted decipherment, the reciprocal nature of Enigma made it possible to use links in either direction - cipher text to crib or crib to cipher text - to form a sort of daisy chain which looped back to its starting point.

## DECODES
Deciphered messages.

## DISCRIMINANTS
Three letter labels (the last three of initial five letter dummy group) indicating the Enigma setting being used. Each setting could be recognised by the use of any one of four different combinations of the three letters allocated to it.

## DUDS
Messages that were sorted into the pile for a setting that was broken but failed to come out in the decoding room or made no sense.

## ENIGMA
The cryptographic system based on the Enigma cipher machine. The machine looked rather like a typewriter. It had a keyboard of twenty six letters but no stops, numerals or operating procedures. When a letter was struck, a letter different from the struck letter showed in an illuminated panel. If you continued to type out the clear text and write down what showed in the panel, you got your cipher text. Put the machine back to the original position at the start of the message and type out your cipher text - and you had your clear text.

## EXCLUSIVITY
The fact that in Enigma no letter could stay the same when encoded.

## FINGER PRINTING
A device for identifying message senders by the bleeps of transmitters, invented by Captain Bolitho.

## FISH
Geheimschreiber - generic term for encoded high speed radio teleprinting used for a few urgent high level German messages: particular variants were Sturgeon, used by the Luftwaffe and Tunny used by the Army High Command in the final stages of the war.

## FO
Foreign Office.

## FUSION
Integrating the knowledge from signals intelligence with decodes from cryptography.

## FUSION ROOM
The central unit where decrypted German messages obtained from Hut 6 were compared with the corresponding data extracted by the log readers from the daily radio traffic between enemy stations, thus enabling a complete wartime picture of the enemy order of battle to be constructed.

## GC&CS
Government Code and Cipher School at Bletchley Park.

## GCHQ
Government Communications Headquarters.

HEAVISIDE LAYER
Named after O. Heaviside, another name for the E region of the ionosphere, extending from a height of 90 to about 150 kilometers. It reflects radio waves of medium wavelength.

INDICATOR
A group of three letters indicating where to position the wheels of the Enigma machine at the start of a message thus giving the setting for an individual message or part message.

INTERCEPT STATIONS
Centres where trained intercept operators listened to, monitored and recorded enemy Morse radio traffic.

KEYS
Different types of daily Enigma settings - wheel-order, *ringstellung, stecker*, and discriminants - for different groups and purposes, such as airforce, army etc, which were known by codenames, largely the names of colours: red, blue, brown etc.

LEADS
Revelations in chat of part of the cipher setting, that led to further Enigma breaks.

LIGHT BLUE
Code name for the separate air force key for the area.

LOG
A listing, often on a printed form, used by intercept officers to record enemy Morse signals as they arrived – including frequencies, call signs, preambles and chat, keying, calling, notice and receipt of messages, queries, checks, cancellations etc.

LOG READING
Summarising from the logs the pattern of communication of a 'star' by means of a diagram with arrows giving the direction of messages, a list of message preambles and notes of significant chat. These summaries made it possible to recognise stars and some of the stations on them from day to day even without knowing the call sign system.

LUFTWAFFE-MASCHINEN-SCHLUSSEL
Red - the main air force key.

LUFTGAUMASCHINENSCHUSSEL
Violet - the air force administrative key.

MASEHINENSCHULUESSEL
Enigma machine setting.

MENU
A programme derived from a crib to run on the bombe to search for breaks.

MI8
Military Intelligence 8.

MORSE CODE
Named after its inventor Samuel Morse, a telegraphic code used internationally for transmitting messages. Letters, numbers, etc. are represented by groups of shorter dots and longer dashes, or by groups of the corresponding sounds, dits and dahs, the groups being separated by spaces.

ORANGE
Code name for the key of the SS 'star' to the concentration camps.

PHASING
The number of tap spaces between repeats in an enciphered message – it was used as an aid to breaking.

PRACTICE KEY
A German practice Enigma setting which codebreakers called Blue.

PREAMBLES
The opening sequence of a message consisting of time of origin, urgency prefix (kr) if any, indicator (letters giving the starting position of the encodement) and the number of letters in the message and the first five letter group, including the discriminant.

PRIMROSE
The code name for the air force administrative key for the area .

Q CODE
A system devised by the British before WW1 and universally used in war and peace by wireless operators. It was a long list of three letter words all starting with Q with accepted meanings.

RECIPROCITY
The fact that, on an Enigma machine, coding and decoding were achieved by the same process.

RED
The German Air Force key Luftwaffe *masehinenschuluessel.*

RE-ENCODEMENTS
Messages that are resent with a different code setting from that used in the first place. There were for example re-encodements from one day's setting into the next day's setting. Re-encodements of a message from a key already broken are clearly likely to provide an excellent crib.

REFLECTOR WHEEL
An integral part of the Enigma machine reflecting and redirecting coding signals.

REPEATS
Any part of the message that was repeated to ensure receipt. Repeats provided a strong crib.

RINGSTELLUNG
The position of the rings on an Enigma machine setting.

ROTOR
One of the encoding elements of the Enigma machine – at first three were issued. Then in 1938 the number was increased to five thus increasing possible rotor orders from 6 to 60.

SCORPION
The codebreakers' name for the army/air force liaison key (*fliegerverbindu ngschlussel*).

SETTING
A particular arrangement of the elements of an Enigma machine. The setting for the day was changed at midnight and consisted of *walzen* (choice of rotors), *ringstellung* (position of rings) and *stecker* (cross plugging). There was also a setting for the individual message or part message, consisting of an indicator of three letters, telling where to position the wheels at the start of the message.

SHAEF
Supreme Headquarters Allied Expeditionary Force.

SIGINT
Signals Intelligence.

SILLIES
Obvious give-aways by the German operators of the Enigma ring settings and/or secret indicators. For example, similarity in the open indicators of first messages of the day from different stations could suggest that they had not moved their rotors much since setting the rings.

SIXTA
Section of GC&CS established in November 1943 responsible for traffic analysis of German wireless telegraphy networks other than naval. It incorporated the Central Party and S.L.P. Named from 6 Traffic Analysis.

S.L.P.
Special Liaison Party, a branch of 6.I.S. based at Bletchley in Hut 3 until merged with the Central Party in SIXTA in November 1943.

STAFFEL
Regiment.

STAR SYSTEM
The radio communications system of the German armed forces, whereby all communication went to, from or through the control of the 'star'. Control had no call-sign. It called an outstation by using the same call-sign, which that outstation used to call control.

STATION X
Bletchley Park.

STECKER
Cross plugging of the Enigma machine.

STENCIL
A type of cipher in which the message is written along the rows of a pad that looks like a crossword puzzle form and then the columns are taken out in a pre-arranged order.

UNTERWALZ
Reflector wheel of an Enigma machine

VIOLET
The code name for the air force administrative key, the *luftgaumaschinens chlussel.*

WALZEN
Rotors of an Enigma machine.

WATCH
A round-the-clock response unit. A cryptographic watch was established in Hut 6 and an intelligence watch in Hut 3.

WO
War Office

Y SERVICE
Intercept stations and intelligence officers responsible for the study of enemy radio networks.

# Bibliography

Andrew, Christoper, *Codebreaking and Signals Intelligence*. Frank Cass (1986).

Birch, Frank, *A History of British Sigint, Vol. II*. National Archives (HW43/2).

Copeland, Jack, *Colossus: The Secrets of Bletchley Park's Codebreaking Computers*. Oxford University Press (2006).

Lewin, Ronald, *Ultra Goes To War: The Secret Story*. Hutchinson (1978).

Nunn, Robert G. Jr., *Critical Observations on German Traffic Analysis in SIXTA*. www.codesandciphers.org.uk (2003).

Robertson, K. G., *British and American Approaches to Intelligence*. Macmillan (1987).

Sebag-Montefiore, Hugh, *Enigma: The Battle For The Code*. Phoenix (2001).

Smith, Michael, *Station X – The Codebreakers of Bletchley Park*. Channel 4 Books (1998).

Welchman, Gordon, *The Hut 6 Story*. Allen Lane (1982).

Thirsk, James, *Bletchley Park: An Inmate's Story*. Galago (2008).

*Dossier on SIXTA*, National Archives (HW50/66).

# Author's Acknowledgements

Many thanks to everyone who has helped me in preparing this book; to Jerry for taking it on and for his publishing skills, to my brothers Andrew and Godfrey Webster for their advice, contributions and patient reading and amendments, to Jimmy Thirsk for his early support and his own excellent book; to the staff of GCHQ for their good nature and quick response; to all the helpers at the British Library and the National Archives for answering difficult questions; to Simon Greenish and staff at the Bletchley Park Trust; to Tony Sale for his great website; to my mother (posthumously) for keeping old letters and photos – and lastly to my husband David, who has shared in all the work without complaint and rejoiced in the fun of discovery.

# Joss Pearson

Joss Pearson, Neil's daughter, is known in the publishing world as founder of Gaia Books, the international co-edition publishing house, famous for such books as *The Gaia Atlas of Planet Management*, *The Natural House Book* and *Sivananda Companion to Yoga*. An Oxford scholar, she has worked in publishing all her life. She is married and has two daughters and divides her time between London and Gloucestershire.

# Index